# On
# Waiting

This is a quite remarkable book, a pleasure to read. Not only is it clear and informative but also by turns witty, melancholic and insightful. The book is astonishingly erudite, but wears this learning so lightly and so charmingly that it is both easy and gripping to read.

Robert Eaglestone, *Royal Holloway, University of London*

Within these covers, Harold Schweizer has assembled a world of philosophical and literary musings on the time-tormented suspension of waiting. As we read his learned, lucid essay, an area of everyday experience swims into focus as if for the first time, the sentences on every page filled with an evocative, almost hypnotic charm. *On Waiting* is a deep plunge into the pleasure of thought.

Wendy Steiner, *Richard L. Fisher Professor of English, University of Pennsylvania*

## Praise for the series

**". . . allows a space for distinguished thinkers to write about their passions"**
*The Philosophers' Magazine*

**". . . deserve high praise"**
Boyd Tonkin, *The Independent* (UK)

**"This is clearly an important series. I look forward to receiving future volumes."**
Frank Kermode, author of *Shakespeare's Language*

**"both rigorous and accessible"**
*Humanist News*

**"the series looks superb"**
Quentin Skinner

**". . . an excellent and beautiful series"**
Ben Rogers, author of *A.J. Ayer: A Life*

**"Routledge's Thinking in Action series is the theory junkie's answer to the eminently pocketable Penguin 60s series."**
*Mute Magazine* (UK)

**"Routledge's new series, *Thinking in Action*, brings philosophers to our aid . . ."**
*The Evening Standard* (UK)

**". . . a welcome series by Routledge"**
*Bulletin of Science, Technology and Society* (Can)

**"Routledge's innovative new 'Thinking in Action' series takes the concept of philosophy a step further."**
*The Bookwatch*

HAROLD SCHWEIZER

# On Waiting

Routledge
Taylor & Francis Group
LONDON AND NEW YORK

First published 2008
by Routledge
2 Park Square, Milton Park, Abingdon, Oxon OX14 4RN

Simultaneously published in the USA and Canada
by Routledge
270 Madison Ave, New York, NY 10016

*Routledge is an imprint of the Taylor & Francis Group, an informa business*



Typeset in Joanna MT and Din by
RefineCatch Ltd, Bungay, Suffolk
Printed and bound in Great Britain by
TJ International Ltd, Padstow, Cornwall



*British Library Cataloguing in Publication Data*
A catalogue record for this book is available from the British Library

*Library of Congress Cataloging in Publication Data*
Schweizer, Harold, 1950–
On waiting / Harold Schweizer.
p. cm.—(Thinking in action)
Includes bibliographical references and index.
1. Waiting (Philosophy) I. Title.
B105.W24S39 2008
128'.4—dc22
2007047201

ISBN10: 0-415-77506-X (hbk)
ISBN10: 0-415-77507-8 (pbk)
ISBN10: 0-203-92715-X (ebk)

ISBN13: 978-0-415-77506-9 (hbk)
ISBN13: 978-0-415-77507-6 (pbk)
ISBN13: 978-0-203-92715-1 (ebk)

# Preface

This is a book about waiting. It is not a philosophy of time, nor a historical survey of cultural attitudes toward waiting, nor a nostalgic contemplation of an idyllic past when we might have waited more patiently (though that is likely). I approach the subject of waiting from a broadly phenomenological perspective. How do we wait? What happens when we wait? What kind of experience is waiting? Is it an experience of time? If so, what kind of time is it that we experience in waiting? Why does waiting get such a bad rap? In attempting to answer such and similar questions, I consult an eclectic range of texts, mostly literary, some philosophical, as well as a number of artistic images. Although the terminology established in Chapter two, which offers a Bergsonian theory on waiting, is taken up in the following chapters, I hope to use my theoretical terms lightly enough so that each chapter can also be read on its own.

My observations include various scenes of waiting – the famous French philosopher Henri Bergson waiting for a lump of sugar to dissolve in a glass of water, seven-year-old Elizabeth waiting in Elizabeth Bishop's poem "In the Waiting Room," Kate Croy waiting for her father in Henry James's novel *Wings of the Dove*, Penelope at her loom waiting for Odysseus, the parents of a little boy waiting for his recovery from a coma, and a number of other "waiters" – painters, poets, and philosophers among them – as they exemplify particular aspects and qualities of waiting: its mental and bodily dimensions, the relationship between waiting and writing, waiting in narrative prose and lyric poetry, the enchantments of waiting, the gendered implications of waiting, how we wait when we read, how we wait when we linger, how we wait for death. I examine the waiter's experience of the endurance of objects, her disquieting sense of her own material embodiment of time, why we pace, why we compulsively consult our watches when we wait. I discuss waiting with and without purpose, the distracted gaze of the impatient waiter, the lingering gaze of the patient waiter, the different kinds of waiting that one performs with expectation and with hope.

I wish to express my gratitude to friends and colleagues who have helped me to bring this waiting to an end. John Rickard's and Richard Kahn's comments were encouraging in the early stages of this project and so were Pauline Fletcher's responses to my readings, especially of Henry James. In the later stages of this project, Michael Drexler, Gary Steiner, and especially Saundra Morris each offered invaluable critical feedback. Thanks also to my exceptionally efficient graduate assistant, Dan Heuer, who spent a good amount of time waiting in front of my office door. I owe much gratitude to Katryn Sandler for her extensive, careful work on bibliographical matters and for her clear-sighted and extremely valuable comments on the entire manuscript.

My thanks go also to the faculty members in the departments of English and French at the University of Tours in France who invited me to give a talk on waiting, the participants of the Graduate Summer School of Literature and Literary Theory in Karlskrona, Sweden, especially its host Danuta

Fjellestad, the organizers and attendees of the annual conference in Medical Humanities, *Making Sense of Health, Illness and Disease*, in Oxford, especially Rob Fisher, and my colleagues at Bucknell who patiently attended the Faculty Colloquium where I presented a theory of waiting.

I extend my thanks to the editors of *Soundings* for permission to reprint a revised version of "Penelope Waiting," which appeared in *Soundings* 85.3–4 (2002): 279–299, and which became Chapter four, "Penelope's Insomnia." My thanks to the editors of *University of Toronto Quarterly*, where some parts of the present Chapters two and three appeared, reprinted by permission of University of Toronto Press Incorporated (www.utpjournals.com), © *University of Toronto Quarterly* 74.3 (Summer 2005), 777–792; and to the editors of *Journal of Modern Literature* © Indiana University Press 2005, who published an earlier, considerably different version of Chapter five under the title, "With Sabbath Eyes." Thanks also to Frédéric Ogée and Maurice Géracht, editors of *Interfaces*, for publishing an earlier version of my work on Ferdinand Hodler. Thanks to Vasiliki Fachard, editor of *Journal of the Short Story in English/Les Cahiers de la Nouvelle* N° 43, (2004) © 2004 by Presses de l'Université d'Angers, and to Peter Twohig and Vera Kalizkus, editors of the proceedings of the *Making Sense of Health, Illness and Disease* conference in 2006, where versions of what eventually became Chapter seven appeared. I am indebted to these people, venues, and journals for their hospitality and for their invaluable feedback on my writing. Finally, I am very grateful to the readers at Routledge for their critical comments and their suggestions, and especially to Tony Bruce for his kind generosity in allowing me to substantially rewrite and revise this entire manuscript.

Grateful acknowledgment is made to the publishers who have given permission to use quotations from the following works. Excerpts from Raymond Carver, "A Small, Good Thing." © 1989 by Tess Gallagher. Reprinted with permission of the Wylie Agency, Inc. Excerpts from "The World as Meditation," "The Pure Good of Theory," from *The Collected Poems of Wallace Stevens* by Wallace Stevens. © 1954 by Wallace Stevens and renewed 1982 by Holly Stevens. Used by permission of Alfred A. Knopf, a division of Random House, Inc. and Faber and Faber Ltd © 2006. Excerpts from T.S. Eliot, "The Love Song of J. Alfred Prufrock," *Four Quartets*, "Preludes." Faber and Faber Ltd © 1969. Eight lines from "Islands," as specified, from *The Seven Ages* by Louise Glück. © 2001 by Louise Glück. Reprinted by permission of HarperCollins Publishers. Twenty-one lines from three poems, as specified, from *Meadowlands* by Louise Glück. © 1996 by Louise Glück. Reprinted by permission of HarperCollins Publishers. Excerpts from Elizabeth Bishop's "In The Waiting Room," "Time's Andromedas," "The Monument," "Sandpiper," "Poem," "The Fish," "The Moose" from *The Complete Poems 1927–1979*. © 1979, 1983 by Alice Helen Methfessel. Reprinted by permission of Farrar, Straus and Giroux, LLC. Excerpts from *The Odyssey* by Homer, translated by Robert Fitzgerald. © 1989. Reprinted by permission of Farrar, Straus and Giroux. Excerpts from "Threshold," from *The Vixen*, by W.S. Merwin. © 1998. Reprinted by permission of Alfred A. Knopf, a division of Random House, Inc. Excerpts from Rosanna Warren, "Odyssey." © 2007. Reprinted by permission of Rosanna Warren. Honoré Daumier (Marseille 1808–1879 Valmondois); *The Third-Class Carriage*. ca. 1865; Black chalk, pen, watercolour and gouache on paper; 23.2 × 33.7 cm; Inv.

Nr. 1923.12; by permission of Oskar Reinhart Sammlung "Am Römerholz," Winterthur, Switzerland. Eleven black-and-white photographs of works by Ferdinand Hodler are reprinted by permission of the Image Resources and Copyright Management, Kunsthaus Zürich. © 2007. I am especially grateful to the Oskar Reinhart Museum and to the Kunsthaus Zürich for their generosity.

# Nobody Likes to Wait

# One

Waiting, one says, is boring.

Thomas Mann, *The Magic Mountain*

## WHY WAIT?

The subject of this book – waiting – recalls St. Augustine's remark that "I know well enough what time is as long as nobody asks me what it is."[1] Waiting is as resistant to description and analysis as time or boredom.[2] Although central to the idea of narrative from Homer to Hollywood, waiting is a temporal region hardly mapped and badly documented. As the literary critic Hugh Kenner observed, there had never been a play about waiting before *Waiting for Godot*. Since then, to my knowledge, only three novels have appeared: Maurice Blanchot's *L'Attente l'oublie* (1962), Fumiko Enchi's *The Waiting Years* (1980), and Ha Jin's *Waiting* (2000).

Obscured by its ordinariness as much as by its alleged uselessness, waiting seems to be almost universally denigrated. "It is difficult to enjoy people for whom we have waited too long," observes Adam Phillips in his book *On Kissing, Tickling, and Being Bored*.[3] "Waiting is horrible," exclaims Clytemnestra in Jean Giraudoux's *Électre*.[4] The envious man of *ressentiment* in Nietzsche's philosophy "lingers at the door"; "compelled to wait," he gives it "flattering names," such as patience or virtue.[5] Although insisting that "haste is the enemy of art," Jeanette Winterson concludes, "We feel that poetry should do more than tell us that somebody is waiting in the hall."[6]

In our frantic world of instant messaging, instant credit, instant gratification, the question "why wait?" or the promise "no wait!" seem to appeal to universal agreement. Nobody, we say proverbially, likes to wait. Lacking the charms of boredom or desire,[7] waiting is neither interestingly melancholic nor despairingly romantic. Between hope and resignation, boredom and desire, fulfillment and futility, waiting extends across barren mental and emotional planes. Those who wander in it or through it find themselves in an exemplary existential predicament, having time without wanting it.

Although waiting rooms, train stations, airports, or hotel lobbies are merely to be passed through, I shall argue in this book that waiting is not simply a passage of time to be traversed. Although time is supposed to function like a door or a hall through which we pass unawares, in waiting, the door jams and the hall is endless. The hour does not pass. The line does not move. Time must suddenly be endured rather than traversed, felt rather than thought. In waiting, time is slow and thick. Waiting is more than merely an inconvenient delay. It is more than a matter of time. Waiting has its rewards, as I want to argue here, though these seem perhaps as inconceivable as a visit to a door or a train station. And yet, we might think of waiting also as a temporary liberation from the economics of time-is-money, as a brief respite from the haste of modern life, as a meditative temporal space in which one might have unexpected intuitions and fortuitous insights. Waiting, as the French activist and philosopher Simone Weil advocates, must be relearned as a form of attention.[8]



## TIME IS MONEY

Let me sketch a context for these observations and claims by going back to the beginning of time, so to speak, namely to the mathematician Isaac Newton. In his *Principia* (1687), Newton distinguishes between "absolute, true, and mathematical time," which "flows equably without relation to anything external," and "relative, apparent, and common time . . ., which is commonly used instead of true time."[9] The ever-increasing precision of chronometrical time in the Western hemisphere since the eighteenth century has reenforced the authority of Newton's "true and mathematical time"; time has become a point of reference according to which lives are set and adjusted like clocks. Soon enough, Newton's mathematical time seemed not a human invention but a divine law: "Thus regulated to keep 'God's time,' " as Graham Burnett writes, "virtuous spirits can make their way through the world and remain 'true' to a distant and divine standard"[10] – so true and divine that the adaptation to synchronized time has arguably led to the West's economic predominance in the world. "Through the techniques by which time is measured," writes Sylviane Agacinski, "and through its assimilation as a market value, we can witness the Western hour's hold over the entire world."[11]

But the economic and technical advantages of synchronized time exact their own price. The money economy changed modern life to "evaluating, weighing, calculating and reducing of qualitative values to quantitative ones," as the German philosopher and sociologist Georg Simmel wrote at the beginning of the twentieth century:

> The mathematical character of money imbues the relationship of the elements of life with a precision, a reliability in the determination of parity and disparity . . . in the same way as the general use of pocket watches has brought about a similar effect in daily life.

Rather than becoming masters of their own time, the bearers of pocket watches were mastered by it. But thereby, Simmel explains, they were ideally adapted to modern metropolitan life, which required "detailed and definite arrangements and measurements."[12]

The beginning of the twentieth century is marked by the concept of time as *the* organizing principle, as Richard Beardsworth sums up. The "logics of modernity require a 'reduction' of the experience of time"; "experience is immediately affected today by economic determination."[13] The experience of waiting is not exempt from these determinations. A case in point is sociologist Richard Larson's observation that

> What really matters is the cost of one's waiting experience, not just in money but in frustration, anger and other stresses. If they understood this principle, industries like fast-food chains, banks, and airlines could reduce their customers' anxieties, better manage their own budgets, and even save lives.[14]

The challenge for these industries is to assign an exchange value not just to the *time* of waiting but also to the *experience* of waiting. Frustrations, anger, and anxieties, too, have their price and must be appeased and remunerated not, it seems, for the sake of the person who waits, but for the budgets of the industries. The lives that might be saved appear to be the lives of customers not of people. Like time, they have become commodities. "Money culture recognizes no currency but its own," as Jeanette Winterson puts it; "Money confuses time with itself."[15] What is lost when time is money is the content of time itself, but it is a content that seems inconceivable without economic determinations or measurements by clocks. And yet, it is just such an inconceivable content of time – inconceivable because immeasurable – that marks the faces and bodies of the passengers of Honoré Daumier's image of *Un wagon de troisième classe* (see Figure 1.1).

### *UN WAGON DE TROISIÈME CLASSE*

To place the passengers in Daumier's image into a train compartment implies its own ironies considering that train schedules necessitated the synchronizing of time in the nineteenth century. The class and social distinctions that are reinforced through such synchronizing are here also on display in the marginal social position and low economic status of the person who waits. Time is synchronized only for those who have pocket watches.

Daumier's passengers seem to have fallen out of the divine standards set by Newton's true and mathematical time. Their bodily gestures and facial expressions convey their habitual,

**Figure 1.1** Honoré Daumier, *Un wagon de troisième classe* (Oskar Reinhart Collection)

mechanical resignation to their "third class" status. If they do not display the frustrations, anger, or anxieties that characterize waiting in the age of fast-food chains, banks, and airlines, they wait in a time unrecorded in the industries' ledgers. Daumier's passengers find themselves with a currency – time – that is worthless. Nobody wants it. They cannot exchange their time; they spend it receiving nothing in return; they would kill time if they could.

If Daumier's passengers strike us as hopelessly from a bygone era, the superficiality of such an impression would belie the fact that waiting is still assigned to the poor and powerless so as to ritualistically reinforce social and political demarcations. The word "wait" or "waiting" occurs numerous times, for example, in Martin Luther King's "Letter from Birmingham Jail." "For years now," he writes, "I have heard the word 'Wait!' It rings in the ear of every Negro with piercing familiarity. This 'Wait' has almost always meant 'Never.' "[16] The poor will always be with us; the poor will always wait. Their time is not money. Daumier's passengers don't travel. They just wait to arrive.



## THE LIGHT OF SPEED

"*What will we wait for when we no longer need to wait to arrive?*" asks social theorist Paul Virilio: "*we wait for the coming of what abides*" (Virilio's italics) – and what abides will be the unceasingly available instant that no longer has to be waited for.[17] For Virilio, post-modernity is characterized by an ever-accelerating contraction of duration: we no longer live in linear time but in the "light of speed." The light of speed is not the speed of light but rather the light that speed emits as, for example, when images flash across a screen. We don't wait for them. Laptops, Blackberries, cell phones, iPhones are to deliver information without making us wait. In a recent issue of *Newsweek*, Robert J. Samuelson even deplores the extinction of the comma that once indicated a pause. "[T]he comma's sad fate is," he writes, "a metaphor for something larger: how we deal with the frantic, can't-wait-a-minute nature of modern life. . . . We don't have time for that. No pauses allowed."[18]

In a culture where "the light interval overrides the classical intervals of extension and duration," where "the old pendulum movement and clockwork mechanisms, as well as the throbbing of quartz watches, are thus giving way to the movement of the [camera's] shutter . . .",[19] we no longer need to wait. "With acceleration," Virilio declares, "there is no more here and there, only the mental confusion of near and far, present and future, real and unreal. . . ."[20] What happens no longer happens as an event arriving in time; it happens in its evanescence, in its momentary coming to light, in its flashing up.

My litany of "no-longer's" and "no-more's" relegates the passengers in Daumier's *Un wagon de troisième classe* to a time manifestly before Virilio's transportation revolution. They still wait to arrive. For them, as for those for whom Martin Luther King speaks, waiting almost always means never. And for those of us who still use commas, speed is still a function of time. Waiting in Virilio's futuristic modernity will now seem paradoxically longer because of the speed by which it has to be accomplished. The indignities of waiting in a culture of the instant, in other words, are also the discomforts of being out of sync with modernity, with the "light of speed," the "habit of velocity," "the moment of the gaze."[21] If technological acceleration increasingly compresses space, for the person who waits, space tediously expands and time slows down. If acceleration of social change leads to a contraction of the present, in waiting the present is painfully prolonged. If the acceleration of the pace of life intensifies experiences,[22] waiting seems only to diffuse them. In short, the temporality of modernity is sudden, instantaneous, like the movement of the camera's shutter, while in the experience of waiting, space and time expand to flat, tedious dimensions. The acceleration of time in modernity, in other words, has greatly accentuated the tediousness of waiting. Waiting seems neither modern nor post-modern – modern having its roots in the Latin *modo*, meaning "just now," which is manifestly not what waiting is.

By the divine standards of time's exactitude, by the diviner economics of its consumption, by the light of speed, waiting must seem a temporary aberration, an anachronism, an embarrassment. The person who waits is out of sync with time, outside of the "moral" and economic community of those whose time is productive and synchronized or whose time need not – in the habit of velocity – be experienced at all. The waiter's enforced passivity expels him from the community of productive citizens; his endurance of time estranges him from the culture of money and speed.

The denials of waiting and the distractions by which it can be forgotten – the magazines in waiting rooms, the entertainment on television, the computer games, the snacks, the cigarettes – amount to a lucrative industry. Ann Barr Snitow writes in her article "Mass Market Romance: Pornography for Women is Different": "While the heroine waits for the hero's next move, her time is filled by tourism and by descriptions of consumer items: furniture, clothes, and gourmet foods.[23]" What is to be avoided at all cost – pun intended – is the experience of waiting.

What has been so enduringly scandalous about Samuel Beckett's *Waiting for Godot* is that it is a play about waiting. But that is perhaps already claiming too much. The play is not *about* anything, not strictly speaking *about* waiting, certainly not about *Godot*. Rather, the play *enacts, performs, requires* waiting. One will have to wait, as Vladimir taunts the audience halfway through the first act: "Charming evening we are having. . . . And it's not over. . . . It's only beginning." Thus, we enact the play as well when we watch it. We, too, do nothing but wait, being "settled numbly in our ritual of waiting," as Hugh Kenner puts it.[24] And we know what to expect: Godot will not come. "One knows what to expect," says Estragon; "No further need to worry," says Vladimir; "Simply wait," says Estragon.[25] But Beckett's critics, as we shall see, greatly worried about Godot.

Only a rarified circle of avant-garde artists received the play with enthusiasm when it came out in 1953; the general public, especially in the United States, reacted with "bewilderment and distaste."[26] One of the play's early American reviewers summarizes the play as a dialogue between "two tramps who inform each other and the audience at the outset that they smell. It takes place in what appears to be the town dump. . . ." The same reviewer doubts that she had "seen a worse play," and charges that *Godot* only demonstrates how "certain intellectuals are capable [of] embracing obscurity, pretense, ugliness and negation. . . ."[27] Even Norman Mailer, otherwise given to progressive tastes, calls admirers of *Godot* "intellectual snobs of undue ambition and impotent imagination."[28] In one of the first reviews of the play, avant-garde novelist Alain Robbe-Grillet declares (with tongue in cheek), "such waiting interests no one." For a conventional audience, he claims, Beckett's play "does not possess, as waiting, the slightest stage value. It is neither a hope, nor an anguish, nor even a despair. It is barely an alibi."[29] Echoing Robbe-Grillet, Robert Champigny comments in a *PMLA* article of the 1960s:

> In Beckett's play, it is waiting that shows existential reality; not waiting for this or that, but waiting; not Time as a form of cognitive thought, but the wait as lived, out of time; not hope or desire or fear, but undifferentiated waiting. This wait is the basic way to live what-has-to-be-lived, the gerundive aspect of existence. Thus, there can be neither optimism nor pessimism, since life must be lived, and that is all. If life makes no sense, it is because life *is* sense.[30]

But Champigny's ascetic reduction of waiting to "what-has-to-be-lived" might inadvertently present Vladimir's and Estragon's waiting as the kind of valiant stoicism that they quite ostensibly spurn. And yet, "all those noble, affirmative elements with which philosophy adorns that existence that Hegel already called 'foul' (*faul*)," as Theodor Adorno writes,[31] are perhaps impossible to resist. Foul or not, life as mere waiting, as simple endurance, is hard to fathom without filling it with tourism and furniture, without assigning it some "Godin . . . Godet . . . [or] Godot," as Pozzo (owner of a pocket watch) proposes.[32] How, then, to think about waiting – waiting as such – just waiting? How can one "simply wait"?

Although Joyce, Proust, Woolf, and Eliot had each introduced "the gerundive aspect of existence" in their own ways more than three decades earlier, the novelty of *Godot*, as Hugh Kenner points out, was that nobody had ever written a play about waiting before, even though waiting, of course, had always been a necessary part of narrative or dramatic development. But that was instrumental waiting, waiting with a purpose, waiting for a denouement, a disaster, a death, for example. The kind of waiting an audience witnessed and shared in *Agamemnon*, Kenner goes on, was directed towards an end, "the inevitable," which was foretold and expected – Agamemnon's death, Orestes' revenge.[33] Electra, who finds waiting "terrible" in Giroudoux's play, asks despairingly, "waiting for what?" but the object of her waiting is thus already announced, the play will reach its closure in the coming of Orestes. We, on the other hand, know – even first audiences knew – that Godot would not come. What then is the difference in waiting between these two, shall we say, traditions? The difference can't be in the fact that Orestes will come and that Godot will not, for either of those endings is inevitable.

The novelty of waiting in *Godot* is not, I suggest, in how we *pass through* waiting but how we *are in it*, not in the expectation of the end of waiting but in the *quality* of waiting as such. If we wait differently in *Godot* than we wait either in clock time or in *Agamemnon*, it is because we "simply wait." Waiting in *Waiting for Godot* is without the preposition "for." And yet, as I have said, it is difficult to conceive of waiting in *Waiting for Godot* without invoking, conceptualizing, indeed expecting Godot – even the Godot who won't come, even the Godot under erasure. For, how can we wait without invoking Godot as a makeshift remedy for the endlessness of waiting? How, in other words, could we *wait* in *Waiting for Godot* without waiting *for Godot?*

Not surprisingly, rather than the experience of waiting *as such*, the identity of Godot quickly became the focus of critical attention and led to an industry of interpretive over-determinations – even though, as Kenner points out, such waiting as we share it in *Godot* is utterly ordinary: ". . . everyone, everywhere, has waited, and wondered why he waited."[34] Vladimir seems to confirm this seemingly universal ordinariness of waiting: "We are no longer alone, waiting for the night, waiting for Godot, waiting for . . . waiting"; he stammers to name an indeterminate, objectless waiting from which Godot has suddenly, in the ellipsis of his sentence, been dropped. "All evening," he goes on, "we have struggled, unassisted. Now it's over. It's already tomorrow."[35] That would be nice, we think. But it's not over, it is tomorrow, and they are still waiting.

When we say that in *Godot* we just wait, we mean that waiting has been emptied of all practical, philosophical, or theological resonance. Beckett's genius is simply to make waiting nothing more than time, just as Henri Bergson's comparable genius, as I will claim in this book, is to make time nothing more than duration. What Vladimir and Estragon wait *for* is perhaps only to get to – and to get us to – this literalism of waiting, to experience their waiting first and foremost, and perhaps ultimately, as nothing other than the endurance of time. For this is not waiting for something that would validate, cancel, or fulfill waiting. This is the kind of waiting we fear that waiting – or living – might amount to: just waiting.

They just wait. Nothing is left but time. They have become time passing, vessels of time, time's bodily manifestations. We are "empty *personae*," as Theodor Adorno puts this, "through which the world can truly resonate."[36] It is this emptiness of substance and yet this resonance of time that hovers in Vladimir and Estragon's gestures. They are waiting. How long, one might vainly ask, are they waiting for Godot? How long until the curtain falls? How long until Godot comes? But even if Godot had come, they would have kept on waiting. "Personally I wouldn't even know him if I saw him,"[37] says Vladimir. When the curtain falls they will keep on waiting: ". . . behind this veil of gentleness and peace night is charging," says Pozzo, "[*Vibrantly*], and will burst upon us [*Snaps his fingers*] pop! like that! [*His inspiration leaves him*] just when we least expect it."[38] But Pozzo's apocalyptic fantasy fades instantly. What we least expect is that they – that we – just keep on waiting.

# A Brief Theory of Waiting: Henri Bergson's Lump of Sugar

# Two

But, you may say, who has long hours for a book these days? The answer must be whoever wants to read one. A reader must pick up a book, then the reader must pick up the beat. At that moment the clock is stopped. Now I am getting his beat into my brain (the rhythm is the main thing in writing).

Jeanette Winterson, *Art Objects: Essays on Ecstasy and Effrontery*

## THE WAITER'S ENDURANCE OF TIME

Henri Bergson's (1859–1941) philosophy of time, famous in Europe and America around the turn of the nineteenth to the twentieth century and now increasingly rediscovered, will prove useful if we want to pursue the question in what time we find ourselves when the clock is stopped. Can such a time be known at all? Can it be known without immediate recourse to the measurements of the clock? Bergson, as we shall see, offers answers to both questions: the question what time is when clocks are stopped, and the question how we can know time without measuring it.

Contrary to Newton, Bergson argues that science "cannot deal with time and motion except on condition of first eliminating the essential and qualitative element – of time, duration."[1] "The mathematician," he writes elsewhere, "will not have to occupy himself with [time], since he is concerned with the measurement of things, not their nature."[2] In his first book, *Time and Free Will*, Bergson thus proposes the existence of two temporalities: one thought and one lived, time and duration. In doing so, Bergson turns the question of proof upside down: the clock, he says, gives us not a sense of time but only a sense of spatial abstractions. To know what duration is requires deeper knowledge, experience rather than spatial measurements.

In order to demonstrate the existence of a time other than abstract, mathematical time, Bergson performs a little experiment:

> If I want to mix a glass of sugar and water, I must, willy-nilly, wait until the sugar melts. This little fact is big with meaning. For here the time I have to wait is not that mathematical time which would apply equally well to the entire history of the material world, even if that history were spread out instantaneously in space. It coincides with my impatience, that is to say, with a certain portion of my own duration, which I cannot protract or contract as I like. It is no longer something *thought*, it is something *lived*. It is no longer a relation, it is an absolute. What else can this mean than that the glass of water, the sugar, and the process of the sugar's melting in the water are abstractions, and the Whole [*le Tout*] within which they have been cut out by my senses and understanding progresses, it may be in the manner of a consciousness?[3]

I find this frequently quoted passage extraordinarily difficult, perhaps because Bergson is saying the obvious: that in waiting we experience time. But what does this mean? Let me try to answer this question by reading the complex process of waiting that Bergson describes in this passage. "I must, willy-nilly, wait," he says, until the sugar dissolves. "*J'ai beau faire,*" reads the French text, "*je dois attendre que le sucre fonde.*"[4] We can translate this as "I can't help it, I must wait . . ." or

"Like it or not, I must wait . . ." or "I must wait, willy-nilly," all of which suggests that the time of waiting is entered with reluctance and resistance. The adverb "willy-nilly" translates this reluctance and resistance felicitously, implying the waiter's vacillating "will I, nill I – I am willing, I am unwilling." Bergson eventually names this vacillation "impatience." In other words, we experience time only then when it is not exactly calibrated to the will, when it is other than, or in conflict with, how we *thought* time should run. Time should run so that we don't have to think of it.

Conscious time "coincides . . . with a certain portion of my own duration." But one's "own duration" is not easily surrendered to scrutiny. What is duration? Though "lived," it seems strangely beyond the waiter's "thought." How is he then conscious of it? How does he feel it? The answer seems to be in the waiter's thwarted desire to "protract or contract" duration. He would "like" to lengthen or shorten, that is measure and adjust, his duration to accommodate it to his desire. But it is precisely in the thwarting of this desire that the waiter becomes conscious of duration; it is something *other* than what can be measured or thought. The time that is felt and consciously endured seems slow, thick, opaque, unlike the transparent, inconspicuous time in which we accomplish our tasks and meet our appointments. We still don't know what duration is. But we might agree that waiting is more than a certain amount of time, more than what can be lengthened or shortened, more than what we *think* it is.

When Bergson notes that his experience of waiting is of a time that "I cannot protract or contract as I like," he is saying the same as that such an experience of duration "is no longer a relation, it is an absolute." In waiting, in other words, time no longer seems to serve as transparent medium or instrument, it is no longer something external *to which* the waiter could refer, *from which* he would be separate, *of which* he could avail himself, *through which* he could pass to accomplish something, as when one takes a leisurely hour to have lunch. In waiting, the hour cannot be turned into lunch; the waiter must live the hour, feel it, embody it, perform it willy-nilly, in his characteristic vacillation which manifests itself, as we shall see, in his agitation, his pacing, his glances at his watch, his fixation on objects.

The hour is intensive not extensive, felt not thought, embodied not applied. The waiter is the embodiment of the hour; it has taken possession of him. Like the lump of sugar, the waiter has become time's unfolding, its manifestation. He *must* wait. Rather than he seizing it – as when he would seize that hour to eat lunch – time has seized him. "It is we who are passing when we say time passes," Bergson writes in *Duration and Simultaneity*.[5] In saying that he cannot protract or contract time "*à volonté*,"[6] as he would like, Bergson states the obvious: that the person who waits cannot defer or prolong, shorten or lengthen – his being.

In waiting, the waiter thus feels – impatiently – his own being; it is a feeling of the un-measurable, perhaps the immeasurable, that which cannot be protracted or contracted. Time "is no longer a relation, it is an absolute." There is no escape from it. The waiter waits in the time that he *is*, willy-nilly. He waits, he vacillates, he wills it – he wills it not, he paces, he looks at his watch. His pacing performs the conflict implied in his impatience. His pacing is to his body what the stirring of the water is to the sugar. If the stirring of the water is to accelerate, indeed to terminate, duration in a desired object, pacing enacts the waiter's desire simply to walk away from the body that endures – the body whose endurance is always also a reminder of its mortality.

## THE MUSIC OF WAITING

Experiences of waiting lead to what Bergson might call enlarged perceptions[7] – partially conscious, partially fragmented, willy-nilly – of the strange phenomenon of our own existential enduring. In waiting, such intuitions of enduring, because they are intimate, are vexingly uncomfortable. We fidget, we pace, we complain, we consult our watches. "We have no interest," writes Bergson, "in listening to the uninterrupted humming of life's depths. And yet, that is where real duration is."[8]

On several occasions, Bergson compares the experience of "pure duration" to a musical phrase that we can only hear if we hear it as an integral whole without consciousness of its individual parts: ". . . we perceive them [the notes] in one another . . . their totality may be compared to a living being whose parts, although distinct, permeate one another just because they are so closely connected." "The proof," Bergson adds, that the musical phrase has a temporality different from mathematical time "is that, if we interrupt the rhythm by dwelling longer than is right on one note of the tune, it is not its exaggerated length, as length, which will warn us of our mistake, but the qualitative change thereby caused in the whole of the musical phrase."[9] When Bergson, in *Duration and Simultaneity*, takes up the metaphor of the musical phrase once again to illustrate the "fluidity of our inner life," he also repeats that the *immediacy* of our experience of duration is possible only in a state of complete mental absorption; here duration is likened to "A melody to which we listen with our eyes closed, heeding it alone. . . ."[10] In *The Creative Mind*, he similarly writes: "let us listen to a melody, allowing ourselves to be lulled by it."[11]

Listening to a story, as Walter Benjamin explains, requires the same self-forgetful receptivity:

> This process of assimilation, which takes place in depth, requires a state of relaxation which is becoming rarer and rarer. If sleep is the apogee of physical relaxation, boredom is the apogee of mental relaxation. Boredom is the dream bird that hatches the egg of experience. A rustling in the leaves drives him away.[12]

Bergson's and Benjamin's illustrations of what happens when the rhythm of duration is interrupted help us to understand that the experience of waiting differs in important respects both from the mental relaxation in boredom and from the mental absorption of the listener who is lulled by a melody. The waiter is neither entirely self-forgetful nor in a state of complete mental absorption. Neither physically nor mentally relaxed, the waiter listens with her eyes open. A rustling in the leaves has stirred up the dream bird. The enchanted listener opens her eyes and becomes the critical reader. The critical reader closes her eyes and becomes the bored listener. The waiter hovers and shuttles between absorption and awareness, between self-forgetfulness and self-consciousness, between the spell of the story and the spelling of a word.

Let us slow down this vacillation between conscious and unconscious states to observe the waiter in either of her unstable mental locations. On the one hand, the waiter's predicament is comparable to that of the listener who has stirred up the dream bird, who dwells too long on a note, and for whom a melody suddenly becomes a sequence of notes and intervals, or for whom a story becomes a series of incidents and a structure of patterns. "We have, no doubt, a tendency," writes Bergson, "to divide it and to picture, instead of the uninterrupted continuity of melody, a juxtaposition of distinct notes."[13] For the waiter who cannot close her eyes and who has awakened from the lull of her absorption in duration, time is suddenly passing in discrete, tedious intervals marked by her compulsive glances at her watch. But on the other hand, and lest we think that the waiter waits only when she looks at her watch, waiting in the increments and fragments of clock time is precisely not *all* that waiting is. To think of waiting as an experience of discrete incidents only would be to reduce waiting merely to a certain amount of time. But that is not so. From time to time, the waiter is reabsorbed, self-forgetful. She waits with her eyes closed, she lingers, she tarries, she listens to the melody of duration, heeding it alone.

Absorbed by the lull of the melody of duration, the waiter waits in brief, but soon to be interrupted, enchantments. It is only in the moment of the interruption of her enchantment that the waiter perceives the otherness of duration: ". . . if we interrupt the rhythm by dwelling longer than is right on one note of the tune," to repeat Bergson's phrase, the interruption will not reveal the note's "exaggerated length, as length" but something else: a "qualitative change thereby caused in the whole of the musical phrase." The *perception* of this qualitative change – since it is a perception – only occurs at the moment when the waiter opens her eyes and awakens from her absorption in the music of duration. It is in this fleeting moment that the waiter is conscious of her intimate existential duration, of her having lingered in time, of time having lingered in her. Her realization of her duration is as momentary and tenuous as the dreamer's remembrance of his dream.

The waiter's consciousness of duration seems merely retrospective, strangely lagging behind her experience as if the waiter only ever heard the humming of life's depths as a fading melody. Prufrock thus recounts in the *present perfect*: "We have lingered in the chambers of the sea"[14] – a tense in which the melody of duration still reverberates in the present. "[T]*here* we have been," as T.S. Eliot writes in *Four Quartets*, "but I cannot say where. / And I cannot say, how long, for that is to place it in time."[15]

The waiter's momentary intuition of her own duration – as this occurs, for example, when we suddenly, but always only intermittently, hear our heartbeat – is accompanied by a certain uncanny discomfort. We thus might want to consider the waiter's compulsive interest in time's "exaggerated length, as length" as a particular distraction that she seeks in order to *think* and not to *feel*. She does not want to feel her endurance of time; she does not want to hear the music that she is. Eliot's memorable scene of the underground train stopping "too long between stations" evokes this momentary discomfort in the passengers' eerie sense of a strange encounter:

> And the conversation rises and slowly fades into silence
> And you see behind every face the mental emptiness deepen
> Leaving only the growing terror of nothing to think about . . . .[16]

We are "empty *personae*," to recall Adorno's remark, "through which the world can truly resonate."[17] In repeatedly glancing at her watch, the waiter displaces and objectifies the intermittent, uncanny sense of her endurance. She would rather think than feel time. She would rather dwell longer than is right on a note than listen to the uninterrupted humming of life's depths.

### THE WAITER'S RESTLESSNESS

Although waiting cannot be *defined* other than in terms of mechanical time, as an "exaggerated length," it is not to be solely *understood* as length, nor is it solely *experienced* as length. "Below" the time of clocks and schedules that constitute our conventional identity, Bergson writes – echoing the Freudian structure of conscious and unconscious states – "below" the official appearance of "the self with well defined states," below this mere "shadow of the self projected into homogeneous space" run the unceasing "confused, ever changing, and inexpressible" currents of duration. "Language cannot get hold of [duration] without arresting its mobility or fit it into its common-place forms without making it into public property."[18]

"Time is a horse that runs in the heart, a horse / Without a rider on a road at night," as Wallace Stevens writes in his poem "The Pure Good of Theory."[19] The waiter is restless. Even if each step were to liberate the waiter from time, even if each number on the face of the watch were to render time relative to the waiter's wishfully autonomous gaze, his very pacing and stirring perform the movements of time. We are its vessels. It is we who are passing when we say time passes. "Even breathing is the beating of time," Stevens adds. The waiter's glances at her watch should make time relative, so that she could assume a position outside of it from where it could be planned and scheduled, so that she would not "coincide" with it, so that time would turn into something else, a number on the face of her watch, an object in her room: functional, useful, desirable, eliciting a "plan of our eventual actions that is sent back to our eyes," as Bergson defines the object.[20] When the waiter compulsively looks at things – her watch, lumps of sugar, pairs of boots, arms braceleted and white and bare – she wants to act, not to wait.

The waiter who compulsively consults her watch to keep track of the intervals of time seeks to fragment the "integral whole" of duration, to quiet the humming of life's depths, in order to arrest her intimate sense of enduring, in order to turn it into common-place forms.

> Consciousness, goaded by an insatiable desire to separate, substitutes the symbol for the reality, or perceives the reality only through the symbol. As the self thus refracted, and thereby broken to pieces, is much better adapted to the requirements of social life in general and language in particular, consciousness prefers it, and gradually loses sight of the fundamental self.[21]

The waiter's exasperated question "How long do I have to wait?" is not only to assure her of the end of her waiting but also implies her desire to escape her inner duration for the outer certainties of time. The deeper experience of waiting is not in its quantity, not in how long I have to wait, but in the fact – the existential fact – that I am enduring. The familiar complaint of children "are we there yet?" suggests that children, who lack the artifice of distraction, who seem naturally contemplative, might be painfully aware of the impermanence of life.[22] To distract them at all cost is to prevent them from feeling their time. But experiences such as illness or suffering, especially if they have to be endured over long periods of time, make deeper waiting inevitable and force the waiter into intimate existential self-encounters. In short: those who are distracted wait superficially in the dimensions of space, whereas the ill and the suffering wait deeply in the dimensions of duration.

What the waiter, in repeatedly glancing at her watch, wants to repress, as I have noted, is her encounter with "the fundamental self," the self that simply endures. But the waiter's futile attempts, each time when she looks at her watch, to calibrate the intimate temporality of her body to the quantitative multiplicity of clock time only return her – in between her glances – to a time that must be endured rather than mastered, felt rather than thought.[23] Shuttling restlessly between felt and thought time, the waiter's typical restlessness is thus the outward sign of her inward attempt to chase her dream bird – to relax – or to chase her dream bird away – to act. But her relaxation is enforced, her boredom is unproductive, her absorption is distracted, her bodily movements are without purpose or direction. She paces – she does not walk. She is restless – she is not active. She is in conflict with the continuity of her inner life as she is in conflict with the imperatives of official, synchronized time.[24] She must wait, she wills it, she wills it not.

In *Waiting for Godot*, Vladimir performs this restlessness when he enters the stage at the opening of the second act:

> *Enter* VLADIMIR *agitatedly. He halts and looks long at the tree, then suddenly begins to move feverishly about the stage. He halts before the boots, picks one up, examines it, sniffs it. . . . Comes and goes. Halts extreme right and gazes into distance off. . . . Comes and goes. . . .*[25]

And yet, this "anguishing oscillation that is 'waiting,' " as Lawrence Harvey calls it,[26] is also productive. In *The Creative Mind*, Bergson defines the philosophical impetus in similar terms to what I have described as the waiter's willy-nilly-ness, her restless shuttling between time and duration. The philosophical impetus, too, for Bergson arises from a perceived difference between external and internal realities: ". . . in the first case consciousness unfolds outward and externalizes itself in relation to itself in the exact measure to which it perceives things as external to one another; in the second, it turns back within itself, it takes possession of itself and develops in depth."[27] "Let us then go down into our inner selves," Bergson declares, "the deeper the point we touch, the stronger will be the thrust which sends us back to the surface. Philosophical intuition is this contact, philosophy is this impetus."[28] If the waiter experiences a similar passage between two realities, if in waiting we also make contact with an inner self, then waiting may, in its own accidental ways, produce a certain philosophical impetus. The waiter, however, only philosophizes in stops and starts, intermittently and inconstantly. She comes and goes. Now her eyes are open, now they are closed. The waiter – the impatient waiter – is an unwilling student of philosophy. When we wait, we who have no time to philosophize are made philosophers against our will.

### THE WAITER'S THINGS

Things do not have the solidity and permanence by which the waiter hopes to arrest his eerie sense of duration. "Things . . . live by perishing," the German poet Rainer Maria Rilke writes. It is therefore to us, "the most fleeting of all," that Rilke assigns the task of naming and remembering things: "say them more intensely than the Things themselves / ever dreamed of existing." For nothing embodies change, movement, duration, indeed being, more intensely than we, the most fleeting, most temporal, most mortal of all. The more we can say of this being of things, the more truly we "are praising them; transient / they look to us for deliverance. . . ." By invoking things, by invoking "house, / bridge, fountain, gate, pitcher, fruit-tree, window," we might not only enter into them and sense their perishing,[29] but we might learn from them our own perishing. Thus, "praise *this* world to the angel," writes Rilke (my italics), not the "unsayable" world of timeless ideas. "Tell him of Things. He will stand astonished. . . ."[30] What astonishes the angel is that things – unlike angels – have duration, that time is the condition of all material things. In things the waiter looks at time. The experience of duration in waiting is the experience of the time the waiter shares with things.

Bergson's experiment with the sugar in a glass of water proves, as he clarifies on the same page, that duration "is an undeniable fact, even in the material world," and that even if the material world presents itself to us "as if instantaneously unfurled like a fan," it rather "unfolds itself gradually, as if it occupied a duration like our own."[31] In Bergson's experiment, this duration of the material world is run at fast-forward speed. Things usually seem more permanent than lumps of sugar in glasses of water. They don't just dissolve. And yet, that is what things do. They live by perishing. The difference between a waiter and a thing is only that the waiter is conscious of time's "hesitation" and "retardation,"[32] whereas things, blissfully oblivious as they are, seem (but only seem) impervious to duration. They don't seem to endure. But things are only "abstractions" from "the Whole," from that unceasing flux of duration that moves within and brings forth all things, and from which "they have been cut out by my senses." The dense, indifferent solidity of things, their illusory outlines and material permanence, are merely opportunistic projections of the human gaze. The illusory permanence of things, to which we happily succumb in shopping or in fetishizing pieces of art or in wanting expensive jewelry, thus relieves us, for a time, from a consciousness of time that is always also the consciousness of our mortality. "(And the time of death is every moment)," as Eliot pithily notes in *Four Quartets*.[33] Although their dense materiality seems to make them impervious to time – diamonds are notoriously "forever" – things have duration, as Bergson's lump of sugar exemplifies.

When the waiter complains "I don't have time," "I am bored," she repeats Bergson's laconic observation that "I cannot protract or contract [my duration] as I like." I cannot lengthen or shorten duration because I am a thing that endures. "We are the age of our objects and experience our own aging at the same time as theirs," as Sylviane Agacinski writes.[34] Or, as Simon Critchley notes, ". . . when we learn to shake off our delusions of meaning and achieve meaninglessness, then we might see that things merely are and we are things too."[35] Molloy in Beckett's *The Unnameable* thinks of himself as " 'nothing more than a lump of melting wax.' "[36]

But briefly to clarify: since individual objects are artificial abstractions cut out of the whole, Bergson does not think – and nor do I – that an individual is comparable to an individual object: "It would therefore be wrong to compare [a living being] to an object," writes Bergson. Though, I might add, this is precisely what we do in warding off our death by fetishizing the illusory permanence of things: diamonds, cars, golf clubs, Shakespeare's *Complete Works*. "Should we wish to find a term of comparison in the inorganic world," Bergson goes on, "it is not to a *determinable* material object, but much rather to the *totality* of the universe that we ought to compare the living organism" (my italics).[37] Thus,

Bergson insists that we compare ourselves not to the illusory abstraction of a thing, but rather to its essential duration. The analogy between things and human beings is their shared essential duration.

"If we do not dwell on these spatial images," Bergson explains in *The Creative Mind*, "pure change remains, sufficient unto itself, in no way divided, in no way attached to a 'thing' . . ."[38] In what might be one of his most provocative statements, Bergson thus suggests that "reality is mobility itself" and that, strangely, "there is change, but that there are not things that change," and consequently that

> Before the spectacle of this universal mobility there may be some who will be seized with dizziness. They are accustomed to terra firma; they cannot get used to the rolling and pitching. They must have "fixed" points to which they can attach thought and existence.[39]

What Bergson means is that things are only particular manifestations of change, of movement, of duration. For Bergson, as we have noted, things are abstractions from the real – the real being duration – just as representations are abstractions from things;[40] neither a material thing nor an image of it could ever truly represent duration. The numbers on the face of the watch that the waiter compulsively consults might well be such fixed points. The waiter's restless pacing might well be her attempts to keep her balance. She is seized with dizziness.

Beneath their illusory appearance, and though they seem solid and immobile, things are all temporal rhythm, dizzying movement. They live, as Rilke says, by perishing. Things endure. Things merely are. While their solidity and immobility are illusory, their endurance is their very condition of being things. This may strike us, of course, either as absurdly self-evident or as absurdly abstract. But the experience of waiting shows, as we have seen, that this realization dawns upon the waiter (if she heeds the philosophical impetus) who is suddenly conscious of her being – her being not as material fact with a name, address, and social security number, but her self as a manifestation of duration. "It is we who are passing when we say time passes," to repeat Bergson's phrase. Waiting, then, allows for the sudden realization that, like things, we *are*. We are one of them. "Consider the system of images which is called the material world," Bergson notes, "My body is one of them"[41] – and in this sense we have an intuition of duration if only because we realize our fleeting bodies are, like Rilke's perishing things, embodiments of duration.

The duration of the material world is also the waiter's own duration; the slow unfurling of things, their dissolving, their melting, "coincides with . . . a certain portion of my own duration."[42] In the restless commotions of impatience, the person who waits seeks escape from the duration she shares with things. For the waiter *feels* herself as a particular thing among things. She is a sentient thing among insentient things. She is a waiting thing among things that don't wait. The person who waits is always singled out.



## THE WAITER'S GAZE

In *Matter and Memory*, Bergson claims that things are not in themselves, but as we perceive them; they are images that come into view relative to their visual, i.e. spatial, position to the body of the observer. The observer's interest in an object *determines* both his subjectivity and the object's always only partial appearance.[43]

> The images which surround us will appear to turn towards our body the side, emphasized by the light upon it, which interests our body. They will detach from themselves that which we have arrested on its way, that which we are capable of influencing.[44]

Bergson defines our body's interest as "the measure of our possible action upon bodies,"[45] or, as he writes in *Creative Evolution*:

> There is no reason . . . why a duration, and so a form of existence like our own, should not be attributed to the systems that science isolates, provided such systems are reintegrated into the Whole. But they must be so reintegrated. The same is even more obviously true of the objects cut out by our perception. The distinct outlines which we see in an object, and which give it its individuality, are only the design of a certain kind of *influence* that we might exert on a certain point of space: it is the plan of our eventual actions that is sent back to our eyes, as though by a mirror, when we see the surfaces and edges of things.[46]



Bergson's concept of perception as the design of a certain kind of influence recalls the function that Walter Benjamin assigns to the movie camera whose close-up and slow-motion functions replicate the waiter's gaze shifting between perception and suppression, between fixation and indifference, between variations of hard outlines and gliding motions. When Benjamin claims that "Evidently a different nature opens itself to the camera than opens to the naked eye – if only because an unconsciously penetrated space is substituted for a space consciously explored by man," it is precisely such an unconscious space that reveals itself to the eye of the waiter. His *compulsive* eye resembles the *intimate* eye of the camera. Like the camera, the waiter's eye performs what Benjamin describes as "lowerings and liftings . . . interruptions and isolations . . . extensions and accelerations . . . enlargements and reductions"[47] – except that, unlike the camera, the waiter's gaze performs these functions compulsively, without a plan of action.

The inconstancy of the waiter's gaze makes objects appear and disappear – abruptly as the change of the camera's angle. The waiter's sudden interest in lumps of sugar or the foliage on wallpaper elicits his profound recognition of the triviality of what he sees. Gratuitous, accidental, annoying in their distinct outlines, their interruptions and isolations, their enlargements and reductions, objects under the waiter's gaze are both familiar and strange, eminently forgettable and impossible to forget. It might be wrong, as Bergson points out, to compare a living being to an object,[48] but objects resemble a waiter's subjectivity. They are like him. He is one of them: gratuitous, accidental, enduring. They regard him "with a gaze familiar" like the impertinent trees in Baudelaire's famous poem "Correspondences."

A person derives his subjectivity from his relation to objects and "the plan of action" they elicit, as Bergson explains. For the waiter, whose relation to objects is not strategic or purposeful but merely accidental, his subjectivity will appear analogously gratuitous, distinct in outline, cut out of the whole, trivial and unforgettable, enlarged and reduced at once. Like the objects the waiter sees and does not see, he appears to himself once present once absent from his scene of waiting, once in exaggerated particularity, once re-absorbed into the flux of the whole. The waiter's design or plan of action is performed in his restlessness and pacing – which movements embody his duplicitous gaze as paralyzed activity or restless boredom. The waiter's gaze is vexed and distracted, bored and fascinated, intimate and remote, focused and vacant. How does he wait? Willy-nilly, he wills it – he wills it not.

This paradox of the waiter's gaze is beautifully exemplified in Daumier's depiction of the man with the top hat on the left in *Un wagon de troisième classe* who is looking out the window with eyes and bodily inclination signifying a sense of boredom and curiosity at once (see Figure 2.1). The man's gaze is

**Figure 2.1** Honoré Daumier, *Un wagon de troisième classe* (detail) (Oskar Reinhart Collection)

rendered masterfully paradoxical so as to suggest that his curiosity cancels his boredom and his boredom cancels his curiosity.

The waiter's equivocal, self-cancelling gaze is at once indifferent and fixed, contemptuous and envious of things. Our dispersal in fragmented, objectified time makes us, Rilke writes,

> . . . spectators, always, everywhere,
> turned toward the world of objects, never outward.
> It fills us. We arrange it. It breaks down.
> We rearrange it, then break down ourselves.
> Who has twisted us around like this, so that
> No matter what we do, we are in the posture
> of someone going away?[49]

This, then, is the posture of what Bergson calls the "insatiable desire to separate," by which the self is "refracted, and thereby broken to pieces." "Rilke's "*Wartender*" in his poem "Turning-Point" enacts this self-fragmentation, this twisted posture of someone always taking leave, in the mental and physical unrest of the person who exemplifies the failure of identification with the endurance of things – and thus the failure of identification with *his* endurance. He is thus *ein Wartender*, a waiter who is not at home in his world, who does not dwell in his mortal body. He is "a waiter, far from home": "*Wenn er, ein Wartender, sass in der Fremde . . .*"

> When he, who was to wait, sat far from home;
> the inn's distracted, averted room
> irritating around him, and in the avoided mirror
> the room again
> and later from the tormenting bed
> again . . .[50]

Like the body in Bergson's philosophy whose "image occupies the centre" and by which "all the others are conditioned," this room is structured by the waiter's un-centered, un-homed, *unheimliche* identity; his sense of self is irritating, reflected in the averted mirror, and again reflected in the waiter's view from the bed. This is "*die geschautere Welt*," the seen world, the world of objects we arrange and which breaks down again, and which breaks us down, and whose echo in us, to use E.M. Cioran's words, is "of time tearing itself apart."[51] Rather than being at home in his merely temporal world, rather than merging with what Bergson would call the unceasing movement of time that becomes temporarily visible, or deceptively substantiated, in things,[52] Rilke's waiter is reflected, refracted, fractured, cut out of the whole like a lump of sugar, like a lump of melting wax; he is himself a tedious reiteration of separate, discrete instances, hence the repetitive accounting of the waiter's room and the things therein.

## In the Waiting Room

# Three

In Worcester, Massachusetts,
I went with Aunt Consuelo
to keep her dentist's appointment
and sat and waited for her
in the dentist's waiting room.

Elizabeth Bishop, "In the Waiting Room"

Over and above all the individual rhythms of music, pictures and words, is the rhythm of art itself. Art objects to the fakeries of clock culture.

Jeanette Winterson, *Art Objects: Essay on Ecstasy and Effrontery*

### ELIZABETH WAITING

Three days shy of her seventh birthday, Elizabeth waits for her aunt who has a dental appointment. Bishop's matter-of-fact description of the place, time, and occasion provides all the "fixed points" to which one can attach thought and existence lest one be seized with dizziness. For halfway through the poem, reading *National Geographic*, Elizabeth suddenly exclaims how strange it is to be "an *Elizabeth*." It is as if she had suddenly stumbled upon what Bergson calls "the precise point where there is a certain intuition to seize on."[1] As she finds herself among things, "grown-up people, / arctics and overcoats, / lamps and magazines," Elizabeth's reaction exemplifies the sudden clairvoyance of the waiter who realizes the astounding particularity of her self in the dizzying movements of duration:

. . . I felt: you are an *I*,
you are an *Elizabeth*,
you are one of *them*.
*Why* should you be one, too? . . .[2]

The critical word here seems to be the indefinite article "an," which points to Elizabeth's sense of the gratuitousness of her own appearance among arctics and overcoats, lamps and magazines. Grown-up people are indefinite articles as well; they are listed among objects; their subjectivities, cut out from the whole like lumps of sugar, dissolve into:

. . . shadowy gray knees,
trousers and skirts and boots
and different pairs of hands
lying under the lamps.
I knew that nothing stranger
had ever happened . . .

Elizabeth's eye here recalls Benjamin's camera, whose intimate perspectives allow the "lowerings and liftings . . . interruptions and isolations . . . extensions and accelerations . . . enlargements and reductions" by which these objects and body parts appear as the strange "unconsciously penetrated space" that opens itself to the gaze of the waiter. The whole within which they have suddenly been cut out is the whole that "held us all together / or made us all just one." Elizabeth encounters the whole in *National Geographic*, whose illustrations of overflowing volcanoes, horrifying breasts, a dead man on a pole represent the primordial reality of duration within which one may appear accidentally as a pair of hands, or as an *Elizabeth*.

Elizabeth's existential surprise at being "an *Elizabeth*" is finally summed up in the waiter's characteristically indignant question: "How had I come to be here, / like them . . .?" It is not least from this question that the waiter seeks relief by being recalibrated into the officially legitimized world of dates and appointments. The poem ends with the lines ". . . it was still the fifth / of February, 1918" – *terra firma*, time as sharable public property, the fixed points to which we can attach thought and existence, all of which makes us forget how we had come to be here, like them, in our fortuitous ways.

### KATE CROY WAITING

My chief example to illustrate the qualities I have been describing – the waiter's agitation, her pacing, her fixation on individual objects, her gaze, her uncanny sense of an inner duration – is from Henry James's *The Wings of the Dove*. "She waited, Kate Croy, for her father to come in, but he kept her unconscionably . . ." reads the first sentence of the book.[3] Kate paces in and out of the waiting room in the "sordid lodgings" where her father has a room "which she knew to be above the one" in which she waits for him.[4] Determined not to "add the shame of fear, of individual, personal collapse, to all the other shames," she steps onto the balcony, she steps back into the room, vexed at having determined to risk fortune and honor to share her small inheritance with her impecunious scoundrel of a father.[5] "Each time she turned in again, each time, in her impatience, she gave him up, it was to sound to a deeper depth, while she tasted the faint, flat emanation of things, the failure of fortune and of honour."

"[C]hanging her place, moving from the shabby sofa to the armchair upholstered in a glazed cloth that gave at once – she had tried it – the sense of the slippery and of the sticky

. . .," Kate Croy tastes "the faint, flat emanation of things." Pacing onto the balcony "to feel the street," turning back into the room "to feel the room," stepping towards the table "to feel the table-cloth and . . ." leaning closer, "the centre-piece and the lamp," Kate in her movements recalls Bergson's claim that discrete objects are perceived to elicit a plan of action. But Kate's pacing only enacts the impossibility of such action. Her impatience is her impotence to transform perception into action. Her consciousness of her duration is her inability to act other than by pacing. The discrete objects of her surroundings are as trivial as lumps of sugar or as foliage on wallpaper, but they acquire, under Kate's camera eye, vexingly distinct outlines. They "tarry" in her brain just as does the note on which the listener dwells too long. Her pacing, though it is a bodily movement, does not amount to an action; her gaze, though it is a perception, does not amount to an interest.

But *precisely* because she is bored, vexed, disinterested, distracted – precisely because she *has no* design, *no* plan of action, the objects in her room tarry in Kate's mind. She dwells too long on them. They hesitate, they resist reintegration into the whole, they are thus momentarily visible in their surprising particularity: the slippery, sticky, glazed cloth, the center-piece, the lamp. Kate's body, to recall Bergson's words, is one of them. How had she come to be here, like them?

Just as the waiter cannot listen to the melody of her inner life with her eyes closed, the room that waiting prepares for her is no longer the ordinary space of functional, invisible objects among which we move blindly, but a location in which objects have acquired uncanny particularity: "She had looked at the sallow prints on the walls and at the lonely magazine, a year old, that combined, with a small lamp in coloured glass and a knitted white centre-piece wanting in freshness, to enhance the effect of the purplish cloth on the principal table. . . ." The waiter forces objects – notes, words, lumps of sugar, sallow prints, lonely magazines – to confess their differences, their particularity, to reveal their distinct outlines, to perform their faint, flat emanations as if they had to justify their capricious existence. Each object is dragged out of its invisibility to have its particularity exposed to the vexed gaze of the waiter who finds in the accidental phenomenology of things only a mirror image of her own accidental presence among them – it "gave her a small, salutary sense, at least, of neither shirking nor lying."

The objects the waiter perceives have been cut out of their habitual context where they would have had function and purpose and where their particularity would have been invisible. But the person who waits sees objects – and in them herself – in their eerie specificity, as the strange thing that a thing is when it is "cut out" of the whole, like pairs of hands lying under lamps, like a lump of sugar dissolving in a glass of water, like a patient etherized upon a table. The fragmentary pairs of hands and shadowy gray knees that Elizabeth discovers, or the "Arms . . . braceleted and white and bare / (But in the lamplight, downed with light brown hair!)"[6] that Prufrock observes with equal fascination, are, like Bergson's lump of sugar, cut out of the whole; they dissolve too slowly.

### THE WAITER'S BODY

An inventory of objects under the gaze of the waiter – the eminently modern waiter here – would have to include the "thousand sordid images" that clutter the waiter's soul in Eliot's "Preludes";[7] the "Stockings, slippers, camisoles, and stays" piled on the typist's divan in *The Waste Land*;[8] "the sallow prints on the walls," and "the lonely magazine" in James's *Wings of the Dove*; the "arctics and overcoats, / lamps and magazines" in Bishop's poem; Ann Barr Snitow's heroine's "furniture, clothes, and gourmet foods"; Vladimir's hat and Estragon's boots in *Waiting for Godot*; and all the objects, fragments, and phrases, scattered, lost, or shored against the ruins of modern texts[9] – texts that are structured, we begin to suspect, by the gaze of the waiter. The objects in these texts are stranded; they resist reintegration into the whole. They hesitate. They defer the consumption of text – the text that tarries in the brain – making the reader wait, making him read the words longer than is right, making him see the objects they name in their grotesque, abstracted particularity. In Beckett's work, these objects cease entirely to offer any distraction from, or direction for, an incurable waiting. In Theodor Adorno's aggrieved words, Beckett's world is reduced to "a stratum of utensils as in an emergency refuge: ice boxes, lameness, blindness, and unappetizing bodily functions. Everything awaits evacuation."[10]

"*My body* is that which stands out as the centre of these perceptions," writes Bergson, "*my personality* is the being to which these actions must be referred." And further on: ". . . in fact I place myself at once in the material world in general, and then gradually cut out within it the centre of action which I shall come to call my body. . . ."[11] But the waiter's body finds itself not in the center but merely *among* objects. His personality is suspended since no actions are referred to him. How had he come to be here? Why should he be one too? The waiter's own body is an estranged object. He is one of them. Himself stranded in time – like a thing – the waiter can no longer delegate his body to a function; he can no longer convert experience into consumable information; he has, to use Bergson's phrase, no plan of action. In Beckett's *Godot*, where Vladimir and Estragon have most conspicuously no plan of action, even their words are stranded objects, fragmented, cut out of the whole, impossible to be reintegrated.

In her essay on waiting rooms in contemporary American fiction, Laura Tanner mentions "the patient's heightened bodily self-consciousness in the medical waiting room" and that the waiting person's seeming bodily integrity "is frequently experienced as a collapse into the powerlessness of pure object status."[12] Such consciousness compels Kate Croy to ascertain her own subjectivity: ". . . and there were moments at which she showed herself, in the glass over the mantel, a face positively pale with . . . irritation. . . ." Such consciousness also accounts for Elizabeth's surprise at finding herself "an Elizabeth."

Just as the waiter waits for the end of her imprisonment in her existential consciousness, so each object is to be released from the gaze of the waiter to resume its invisibility in the universal flux of the whole. Bergson's lump of sugar performs this vanishing act as it dissolves into the transparency of water.



## THE SHADOW OF WORDS

Among the tablecloths, lamps, and clutter of that excessively furnished room in James's novel, we find Kate pausing, looking at herself in the mirror. Among the shadowy gray knees, trousers, skirts, boots, and different pairs of hands, we overhear Elizabeth's sudden, startling self-discovery. Among the stockings, slippers, camisoles, and stays on typists' divans, we glimpse the "self that endures." Beneath the clutter of things and the clamor of words runs the musical phrase of pure duration; beneath the conventions of language resides the "self that endures."

In contrast to James's literary style, our ordinary language "overwhelms or at least covers over the delicate and fugitive impressions of our individual consciousness."[13] What is required to overcome the limitations of ordinary language, Bergson proposes, is "some bold novelist." The complexity and subtlety of the novelist's language, he writes in *Time and Free Will*, have torn aside "the cleverly woven curtain of our conventional ego."[14] Although this novelist "spreads out our feeling in a homogenous time and expresses its elements by words," although his linguistic constraints force him to present our feeling as its mere shadow, "he has arranged this shadow in such a way as to make us suspect the extraordinary and illogical nature of the object which projects it."[15] Or, to say this differently: although he must employ the logic of grammar and the linearity of syntax, the novelist recovers in the virtuosity of his style the fluid processes of duration that constitute "the fundamental self." In his book *The Early T.S. Eliot and Western Philosophy*, M.A.R. Habib offers an example of this style in his comments on Eliot's "The Love Song of J. Alfred Prufrock":



> The "you" and "I" from the poem's beginning have wandered, as if in a dream, beneath the depths of literal language, viewing conventional experiential categories from within their own repressed depth, from within the experiences which exceed that language, as dream exceeds reality.[16]

The rhythms of literary syntax, the allusions of figurative language, the polyphonies of literary form leave a trace of that inward, dreamlike flow of duration that we are when we truly, unconsciously, are ourselves. In this way, Bergson claims, "He [the novelist] has brought us back into our own presence."[17] Or, in Jeanette Winterson's pithy phrase: "Books, like cats, do not wear watches."[18]

The reader who would follow me to such unverifiable conclusions would need to listen with her eyes closed; she would have to put aside the cleverly woven curtain of our conventional ego; she would have to ignore the watch that cats don't wear. Such a reader, to borrow Sylviane Agacinski's description of the *flâneur*, "must be available to time, *to let time pass*, to spend it without keeping count, to know how to waste it. . . ."[19] Listening to, lingering in, the semantic, tonal, rhythmic totality of James's language, the reader-as-stroller, the waiter-as-lingerer, intuits in the shadow cast by words the "confused, ever changing, and inexpressible" aspect of Kate Croy, her "fundamental self," how she endures, how she *is* among and beneath and in spite of the overstuffed conventions of her late Victorian world. It is this confused, incommensurable subjectivity that the bold novelist evokes.

When we read slowly, we wait. We remove the veil, taste the faint, flat emanations of words, sound to a deeper depth. We have lingered with that most hesitant of literary characters, Prufrock, "in the chambers of the sea." We have, momentarily, been brought back into our own presence. "*There* we have been," to repeat Eliot's lines from *Four Quartets*, "but I cannot say where. / And I cannot say, how long, for that is to place it in time."[20]

It seems likely that only a spontaneous, inconceivably authentic language could express the dreamlike, fluid duration that constitutes our inner life. Bergson's novelist would need to be bold. Maurice Blanchot comments on this requisite stylistic virtuosity in that "Bergson had an extreme distrust for words and an extreme confidence in poetry."[21] In allowing the bold novelist – or the bolder poet – to offer glimpses beyond language, Bergson credits literary – poetic – language with a revelatory power to render that uncanny, inward, eerily corporeal sense of duration that we also feel when we wait. "This innocence of profound life," as Maurice Blanchot paraphrases Bergson's *durée*, "this mobility of self that loses itself in an obscure intimacy, this whole pure reality whose spirit no image can represent and that is for Bergson the essence of duration"[22] – this is what Bergson credits as the intuitive, motivating genesis of art. And this is what I propose to trace in the chapters to come.

# Penelope's Insomnia
# Four

I wait, to read the meaning in that beacon light . . .

Aeschylus, *Oresteia*

Is it Ulysses that approaches from the east,
The interminable adventurer? The trees are mended.
That winter is washed away. Someone is moving

On the horizon and lifting himself up above it.
A form of fire approaches the cretonnes of Penelope,
Whose mere savage presence awakens the world in which
she dwells.

Wallace Stevens, "The World as Meditation"

## WAITING TO BEGIN

"Suppose that I am going to recite a psalm that I know," writes St. Augustine. "Before I begin, my faculty of expectation is engaged by the whole of it." Similarly, we find Odysseus at the beginning of *The Odyssey* delayed on the island of Calypso, "scanning the bare horizon of the sea" (5.166)[1] as if it were the blank page onto which he is about to write his story. "All the rest . . . had long returned / while he alone still hungered / for home and wife" (1.19–22). When he sets sail, his waiting enters the temporality of narrative so that, in an Augustinian way, "the province of memory is extended in proportion as that of expectation is reduced, until the whole of my expectation is absorbed" (11.29). Like Homer's *Odyssey*, Aeschylus' *Oresteia* opens with the watchman waiting on the roof of the palace: "I wait; to read the meaning in that beacon light . . ." – which lines announce Agamemnon's imminent arrival and the beginning of the tragedy. Narratives – psalms, poems, plays – engage the faculty of expectation; they emerge out of waiting and, in the course of their telling, structure and transform our time. No story, then, without waiting, and perhaps no waiting that does not harbor a story.

"Home you may not go / unless you take a strange way round . . ." (10.543–44), explains Circe to Odysseus. The strange way round, as I shall propose in this chapter, resembles the motions of the weaver's hands at the loom, for Penelope weaves and waits for her husband's return. Her daily weaving and nightly unweaving, I argue, parallels the delays and detours of Odysseus' journey; it resembles the complicated revisionary processes of writing and all that writing implies: hope, anticipation, impatience, futility, despair. Her daily weaving and unweaving recalls Bergson's distinction between time and duration: during the day Penelope waits in time, during the night she waits in the heterogeneous, mysterious movements of duration. Narratives are woven with threads of time. Narratives are suffused with waiting. A literary text such as *The Odyssey* requires our waiting as well. We, too, weave and unweave, expect and retract, wait and linger as we read.

The end of all such waiting will produce Odysseus' miraculous homecoming and the finished text of *The Odyssey*. But these, I suggest, are only temporary closures of waiting. We will open *The Odyssey* again, Penelope will re-commence her waiting. We will wait again. Literary narratives teach us how to come to the end of waiting and then to wait again, how to weave and unweave our time, how to compose and revise our life. They teach us also that no end, no object of waiting can fulfill our waiting. "Whatever the importance of the object of waiting, it is always infinitely surpassed by the movement of waiting," as Maurice Blanchot puts it.[2] As if to enact the endlessness of this movement of waiting, Odysseus will be restless at the end of *The Odyssey*, planning new journeys and new exploits. What constitutes a literary text or work of art is not its formal closure or aesthetic completeness but rather its continuity in our own time of waiting.

## THE ENCHANTMENTS OF WAITING

Odysseus, stranded on "a wooded island, in the sea's middle" (1.70), absent from the world of mortals, detained by the pleasurable trance of timelessness, waits for the story to begin. Both the remoteness of her island and of Calypso herself, whose name means the "hidden" one and "the one who hides," dramatize Odysseus' exile from the world. "His life may not in exile go to waste" (5.119), exclaims Zeus' messenger Hermes.

But one does not need Calypso's promises of immortality for the illusion of such remoteness from time. Even one who waits for a train, or an appointment, or a phone call experiences, perhaps briefly and fleetingly, the lull of pure duration, the trance of waiting offering the promise of an immortality of sorts if one were to renounce all obligations to the world, if one were not to take the train, not to keep the appointment, not to pick up the ringing phone.[3] "Waiting is an enchantment," writes Roland Barthes, "I have received orders not to move. Waiting for a telephone call is thereby woven out of tiny unavowable interdictions to infinity."[4] It is to such an infinity, such an otherworldly sphere that Hermes carries his message. "Even a god who found this place / would gaze, and feel his heart beat with delight" (5.79–80).

The Greeks, as Louise Glück tells us in her poem "Parable of the Hostages," had encountered this realm of enchantment before, on the shores of Troy:

. . . who once
delays the journey is
already enthralled; how could they know
that of their small number
some would be held forever by the dreams of pleasure,
some by sleep, some by music?[5]

. . . by music, if we recall Bergson's metaphor, to which they would have listened with their eyes closed, heeding it alone. In Glück's *The Seven Ages*, the enchantment of Calypso's island seems intimated in a poem entitled "Island." No names are mentioned. The poem records an intimate moment's "many aspects" and "motion not yet channeled in time . . . the moment / shimmering." Bergson would call it duration not time, not something thought but lived, not measured but endured, for duration is indivisible – "Not changing because time was passing," writes Glück, "but because the one moment had many aspects." Among the moment's many aspects are day and night merging into each other like "Sound of the wind. Sound / of lapping water" which rhythms are repeated in the languid gesture of "a hand moving / backward, then forward"[6] and which motions seem to be indivisible.



When waiting is experienced as enchantment, it happens within time experienced as timelessness, as waves, as rhythm, as melody. Such a waiter resembles Benjamin's self-forgetful person who listens to a story, or Bergson's rapt listener who keeps his eyes closed heeding the music of duration. Such waiting happens without the concept of loss or anticipation, difference or deferral. It is presence. It is time evanescent like wind or fluid like water.

In W.S. Merwin's poem "Threshold," the speaker – a "stranger by himself" reminiscent of Odysseus – reflects such intuitions of that deeper time accessed in the enchantment of waiting:

> and when I turned to look back I did not recognize a thing
>   the sound of flying whirred past me a voice called far away
> the swallows grew still and bats came out light as breath
>   around the stranger by himself in the echoes
> what did I have to do with anything I could remember
>   all I did not know went on beginning around me
> I had thought it would come later but it had been waiting

Poems, particularly of such lyrical, romantic provenance, reveal "all I did not know" – in the realm of an enchantment, a realm which casts its spell just as Bergson's melody does, as Benjamin's story does, as Calypso does with her weaving and singing and loving. Calypso "fed him, loved him, sang that he should not die / nor grow old, ever, in all the days to come" (5.142–143).

But Odysseus has grown tired of Calypso. Even in the spells of enchantment, it seems, things perish, time passes. Even in the enchantments of immortality, one waits. The Victorian poet Augusta Webster renders the weariness of satiety in her poem "Circe" – Circe who lives, like Calypso, in the trance of timelessness:

> I am too weary of this long bright calm;
> Always the same blue sky, always the sea
> The same blue perfect likeness of the sky,
> One rose to match the other that has waned,
> To-morrow's dawn the twin of yesterday's;

And every night the ceaseless crickets chirp
The same long joy and the late strain of birds
Repeats their strain of all the even month;
And changelessly the petty plashing surfs
Bubble their chiming burden round the stones;
Dusk after dusk brings the same languid trance
Upon the shadowy hills, and in the fields
The waves of fireflies come and go the same,
Making the very flash of light and stir
Vex one like dronings of the shuttles at task.
Give me some change. Must life be only sweet . . .?

Calypso's spell, as Jean Pierre Vernant remarks, would have condemned Odysseus to oblivion. Or it might have condemned him to death. If Odysseus can survive only in his story,[7] it is a story poised to rupture "the same languid trance" of the enchantments of waiting. "Time / begins now," we read in Louise Glück's poem "Odysseus' Decision," time

in which he hears again
that pulse which is the narrative
sea, at dawn when its pull is strongest.[8]



## ODYSSEUS' IMPATIENCE

Odysseus waits with the expectation of the writer who is about to tell his story. He scans the horizon. "When someone waits for something," Hans-Jost Frey writes, echoing St. Augustine, "he is entirely fulfilled by what he expects."[9] What Odysseus expects is nothing other than the fulfillment of his waiting, represented by his desire for home and wife. He knows what he is waiting for, and it gives him the power to refuse Calypso's offer. But waiting with expectation, as Frey explains, is "something entirely temporary . . . a state of lack that one wants to overcome as fast as possible."[10] When the story opens at the end of seven years of waiting, Odysseus' impatience is palpable. His impatience is also the writer's impatience which, according to Maurice Blanchot, constitutes the writer's inspiration: "impatience must be the heart of deep patience, the pure bolt of lightning which leaps out of the breast of patience because of its infinite waiting. . . ."[11] Each morning, thus, Odysseus leaves Calypso's cave and goes down to the beach to sit

> in his stone seat to seaward – tear on tear
> brimming his eyes. The sweet days of his life time
> were running out in anguish over his exile,
> for long ago the nymph had ceased to please.
> Though he fought shy of her and her desire,
> He lay with her each night, for she compelled him.
> But when day came he sat on the rocky shore
> and broke his own heart groaning, with eyes wet
> scanning the bare horizon of the sea.
>
> (5.158–166)

Turning towards the sea, scanning the horizon as if the island of Ithaca were to rise out of the air by the sheer power of his impatience (1.79–80), Odysseus embodies the preposition "for," as in "waiting for."

Calypso's promises of timelessness would have removed the preposition "for." Her promise of immortality would have exchanged his stone seat for her soft bed. There he would have lingered without memory or desire, in the languid sweetness that Augusta Webster so aptly evokes. Refusing Calypso's promise, Odysseus takes position on a stone seat to seaward, the position of waiting in its symbolic, psychologically appropriate setting, on the rock whose time is torment.

Time is the rock on which Odysseus waits. It becomes the symbolic place for the one who waits impatiently for the beginning of the story that would remedy his waiting, bring it to an end. To bring this waiting to an end, however, will require the intervention of the gods, for whom, as Vernant writes, "it is the great scandal" to see Odysseus wait.[12] And that is perhaps what stories are supposed to accomplish: they are to transform the endlessness of time to human proportion, to assign waiting a destination implied in the preposition "for." Death and marriage are the major tropes, tragedy and comedy the chief genres, by which such waiting comes to an end. Stories allow us to pretend that there is a cure for waiting.

### PENELOPE WEAVING

Meanwhile, Penelope asks the minstrel to sing of other deeds than "the bitter song, the Homecoming of Akhaians" (1.377), since it opens in her "the wound of longing" (1.393). Upon which she "mounted to her rooms again / with her two handmaids, then she fell to weeping / for Odysseus, her husband" (1.410–412). After seventeen years of waiting, Penelope devises a ruse to keep at bay her numerous suitors and to defer her re-marriage until the shroud for her father-in-law, Laertes, is finished: during the day she weaves, during the night she unravels her work. Penelope's weaving and unweaving represent the public and private aspects of waiting.

After three years, her nocturnal occupations are discovered by her maidservant, who informs the suitors, and Penelope is forced to complete the shroud.

> We found her unraveling the splendid shroud,
> and then she had to finish, willy nilly –

finish, and show the big loom woven tight
from beam to beam with cloth. She washed the shrouding
  clean as sun or moonlight.

(24.163–167)

If weaving measures time, so does making music or writing; each traces the passage of time "from beam to beam," across the lyre, the page, the day. "If this is so, what means do I use to measure time?" asks St. Augustine, and the answer he gives is the syllable, the line, the poem (11.26).

Her ruse discovered, Penelope's waiting is now determined by the parameters of the loom, "from beam to beam." If waiting has a day and a night side, this is its day side: an object-related, purposeful waiting characterized by the patterned and plotted passage of time, the warp and weft of measurable time, performed in the rhythmical or repetitive movements of Penelope's hand across the loom, as it is in the movements of the minstrel's hand across his harp or the writer's hand across the page, each striving to produce a "finished" texture, "woven tight," "clean as sun or moonlight." So one waits in the light of public expectation.

"[Penelope's] weaving, like Helen's has been connected with the Indo-European conception of poetic creativity . . ." as one commentator explains;[13] and another, comparing Penelope to Clytemnestra, remarks that both women are "as clever at weaving a piece of cloth as at devising a plot."[14] Nancy Felson-Rubin argues that Penelope's "epithet *periphrôn* and her name (perhaps from *pênê*, 'woof' or 'loom') suggest that she is the sort of character who actively weaves her life-story . . ." as well as "the multiple plots" by which she teases, thwarts, desires, and rejects her suitors.[15] "Often the 'line' of connection in stories is pictured as a thread," as Margaret

Visser explains, "(The word 'line' itself comes from the Latin *linea*, a flaxen thread for making linen)."[16] Plot and cloth, line and thread, weaving and poetic creativity are here conjoined under the index of waiting, a waiting that is clearly gendered in order to emphasize woman's traditionally central, if invisible, power that weaves, develops, complicates, and draws narratives to their end.

But the gendered aspects of waiting and its analogy to weaving also suggest repressive processes:

> The unpredictability and innate corruptibility of the female character meant that activities like woolworking, as well as having a positive, civilizing aspect, were seen in negative terms as a means of keeping women out of mischief by virtue of a time-consuming series of tasks.[17]

Woolworking can thus be thought of as an early model for a pedagogy later to be assigned to occupations like reading and writing. The activities of weaving, reading, and writing all provide an indubitable, visible, readable account of waiting. They all render waiting accountable, especially woman's waiting.[18]

Such intuitions of the repressive, gendered aspects of waiting are poignantly rendered in Glück's first poem in *Meadowlands*, "Penelope's Song":

> Little soul, little perpetually undressed one,
> do now as I bid you, climb
> the shelf-like branches of the spruce tree;
> wait at the top, attentive, like
> a sentry or look-out. He will be home soon;
> it behooves you to be
> generous.

Irony gives way to anger as Penelope ponders her husband's indiscriminate appetites for "nymphs" and "grilled chicken."

> Ah, you must greet him,
> you must shake the boughs of the tree
> to get his attention,
> but carefully, carefully, lest
> his beautiful face be marred
> by too many falling needles.

In daylight, Penelope's beauty is that of her accountability; it is a public beauty, wrought by weaving "clean as sun or moonlight." When one of her suitors exclaims, "Beauty like yours no woman had before, / or majesty, or mastery," Penelope answers: "Eurýmakhos, my qualities – I know – / my face, my figure, all were lost or blighted / when the Akhaians crossed the sea to Troy" (18.312–317). Penelope's response implies an intimate embodiment of the passage of time, time-as-endurance, invisible to her suitors. They cannot see her endurance of waiting, they cannot see her nocturnal unweaving.

Penelope's weaving, of course, will only confirm the death of Odysseus and Laertes as well as bring about Penelope's marriage, each event signifying the end of waiting and the end of a story. Once it is finished, such waiting will prove to have been purposeful – but at the price of Penelope's "fundamental self" and at the price of Odysseus' and Laertes' lives. In her nocturnal unraveling of the shroud, Penelope not only prolongs their lives by prolonging her waiting, she also preserves her complex, conflicted identity. "She has composed, so long, a self with which to welcome him . . ." writes Wallace Stevens in "The World as Meditation."[19] By complicating, prolonging, and deferring the dreaded signification of her weaving and the consummation of her story in death and remarriage, Penelope's weaving and unweaving represent the complex and contradictory aspects of waiting. Rosanna Warren renders this complexity in her poem "Odyssey":

> Through the strong warp of the past, she shuttles the woof of the
>     future,
> and the fabric of the present tightens into shape. But the present?
> Laertes' death is constantly deferred. Constancy is her *métier*: to
> preserve it, she lets the present unravel at her fingertips, while
>     night
> breathes over her shoulder and complicates the pattern.[20]

The "friction between social time and inner time is always lying in ambush," as Carmen Leccardi points out. "The latter time is basically anarchic (alien to any kind of external constriction), cyclical (as dreams or feelings daily remind us), multi-directional, unrepeatable, and impossible to measure."[21] In waiting that is to be purposeful and object-related, in weaving that is to be "clean as sun or moonlight," Penelope's time loses this dimension of depth. Her story is reduced to a predictable outcome. "Only the nonliterary book is presented as a stoutly woven web of determined significations," Maurice Blanchot notes. "But the book whose source is art has no guarantee in the world . . . ."[22]



### PENELOPE'S INSOMNIA

The shroud is Penelope's public account of waiting. To finish it is hateful to Penelope (2.118). Daily it is tightly woven into forms and patterns; nightly it is reduced to a tangle of threads, when waiting is no longer directed towards the future, but simply endured. Such waiting is not waiting *for something* but waiting for *something to pass*. No text, no cloth, no weaving is there to assure us of the moral or psychological soundness of the person who must have passed through that un-plotted time. "In other words," to repeat Bergson's phrase,

> our perceptions, sensations, emotions and ideas occur under two aspects: the one clear and precise, but impersonal; the other confused, ever changing, and inexpressible, because language cannot get hold of it without arresting its mobility or fit it into its common-place forms without making it into public property.[23]

This second aspect is one of the implications of Penelope's unraveling of the shroud at night. It is a time unaccounted for, a refusal of conventional patriarchal narrative, a refusal of the beauty Eurýmakhos wants to see, a refusal of the luxuries that would distract Penelope from her endurance of time.

It is at such a time that we can imagine Penelope finding herself exposed to the pure, anarchic flow of time before it is structured – each day – into time measured by her weaving. During the day, Penelope waits in what Frank Kermode calls *chronos* " 'passing time' or 'waiting time,' "[24] the time of the repetitive, measurable work of her hands. During the night she waits without end in a heterogeneous duration, confused, ever changing, inexpressible. During the night, Penelope weeps and unravels the texture that would tell of her waiting, that would render it "clean as sun or moonlight." "Through affliction," Maurice Blanchot writes, "we endure 'pure' time, time without event, without project and without possibility; a kind of empty perpetuity that must be borne infinitely. . . ."[25] Stevens imagines Penelope's nocturnal waiting as "an inhuman meditation, larger than her own. / No winds like dogs watched over her at night."

Waiting that is simply to be endured does not have the clarity, tightness, and patterns of the fabric that Penelope is weaving during the day; during the night the threads of time are a tangle: anarchical, cyclical, multidirectional, unrepeatable and impossible to measure, as Leccardi writes. "Let me be / blown out by the Olympians! Shot by Artemis," Penelope cries out on such nights, "I still might go and see amid the shades / Odysseus in the rot of the underworld . . ." (20.89–92), and we do not know if this is the extreme of hope or hopelessness – impossible to measure, impossible to recount. A few lines later, she ends her outburst with the resigned realization that even in her dreams she will be waiting:

> Evil may be endured when our days pass
> in mourning, heavy-hearted, hard beset,
> if only sleep reign over nighttime, blanketing
> the world's good and evil from our eyes.
> But not for me: dreams too my demon sends me.
>
> (20.94–98)



The concealment of such nocturnal despair is dramatically rendered when, on the eve of her first encounter with the disguised Odysseus, Penelope is transformed by Athena into a "beautiful lady" who would cause her suitors "weakness . . . in the knee joints" and hearts "faint with lust" (18.265–266). But in spite of Athena's cosmetic skills, Penelope descends the stairs into the great hall wearily recalling some rare hours of sleep.

> Ah, soft
> that drowse I lay embraced in, pain forgot!
> If only Artemis the Pure would give me

death as mild, and soon! No heart-ache more,
no wearing out my lifetime with desire
and sorrow. . . .

(18.252–257)

Such waiting has none of the outward "majesty, or mastery" with which Penelope appears to the suitors, nor the beauty of the "splendid shroud." Beneath the appearances of beauty's majesty or mastery and within the tight weave of the texture of the splendid shroud are the bold novelist's word-shadows, are the tangles and loose threads that must be concealed by the time the morning comes. Walter Benjamin lyrically dramatizes this suggestion of a Freudian paradigm of unconscious and conscious passages through time. "For here," he writes,

> the day unravels what the night was woven. When we awake each morning, we hold in our hands, usually weakly and loosely, but a few fringes of the tapestry of lived life, as loomed for us by forgetting. However, with our purposeful activity and, even more, our purposive remembering each day unravels the web and the ornaments of forgetting.[26]

While her daily weaving is related to the future as *conscious* memory is to the past, Penelope's nightly unraveling is related to the future as *involuntary recollection* is to the past. Such an analogy, as Benjamin suggests, of Penelope's unraveling to Proust's *mémorie involontaire* enables us to think of her nocturnal waiting as *une attente involontaire*, an involuntary waiting where neither the waited-for object nor measurable time itself seem any longer relevant. Such waiting, then, to follow Benjamin's intimations, would project itself past the end of *The Odyssey* – it would allow Penelope to wait and deceive her suitors forever.

To bring this waiting – and writing – to a conclusion will necessitate intervention: the discovery of Penelope's strategy, which forces her to complete the shroud. Her discovery reinstates a narrative that is opposed to Penelope's desire, that violates her "fundamental self."

Until such things come to pass, Penelope lives not in time but in duration. Here the loose thread of her waiting falls into what Blanchot calls "time of the abyss," or into what Gérard Genette calls *achrony*, a temporal space beyond the coordinates of conscious remembrance or anticipation. To render Penelope's unraveling of her cloth would require the somnambulist style of Proust, who, as Genette claims, "made clear, more than anyone had done before and better than they had, narrative's capacity for *temporal autonomy*."[27] Such enigmatic time is alluded to in Benjamin's reference to "a lost twittering of birds, or a breath drawn at the sill of an open window" which characterize Proust's "hour that was most his own." In his comments on Proust's sleepless nights, Benjamin muses, "there is no telling what encounters would be in store for us if we were less inclined to give in to sleep."[28] If Penelope's nocturnal waiting takes place in the *achrony* in which Proust, Joyce, Woolf, or Eliot writes, do we sense in her insomnia, nightmares, and unraveling a breath drawn at the sill of an as yet unthinkable literary avant-garde?[29]

In his essay "Time and the Novel," Maurice Blanchot describes Rhoda, one of the six characters of Virginia Woolf's novel *The Waves*, in the way we may imagine Penelope's nocturnal waiting as coming

> closest to pure time, to the empty time that is the greatest reality of time, of time outside of the world, outside of things, the time of solitude, time of the abyss that we can envision,

> when it escapes from the abstract, only by the very anguish of time.[30]

Early on in Woolf's novel, we overhear the young girl Rhoda threatened by the same otherworldly time "outside the loop of time":

> Meaning has gone. The clock ticks. The two hands are convoys marching through a desert. The black bars on the clock face are green oases. The long hand has marched ahead to find water. The other painfully stumbles among hot stones in the desert. It will die in the desert. The kitchen door slams. Wild dogs bark far away. Look, the loop of the figure is beginning to fill with time; it holds the world in it . . . and I myself am outside the loop; which I now join – so – and seal up, and make entire. The world is entire, and I am outside of it, crying, "Oh, save me, from being blown for ever outside the loop of time!"[31]

Like Rhoda's, Penelope's nocturnal thoughts are outside the loop of time, from where she returns every morning to her duties at the loom, to the great hall below, and to Homer's heroic tradition.

### PENELOPE'S AMBIVALENCE

"But mortals cannot go forever sleepless" (19.687), Penelope responds to Odysseus, who has meanwhile returned disguised as a beggar. Mortals cannot wait forever. In the next chapter (20) we overhear Penelope's prayer to Artemis. Her allegiance to Artemis, as has been pointed out, strengthens her resolve not to become a Helen or a Clytemnestra "but patiently to await Odysseus' return."[32] Agamemnon's shade had prophesied to Odysseus:

> Tyndáreus' daughter waited, too – how differently!
> Klytaimnéstra, the adulteress,
> waited to stab her lord and king.
>
> (24.224–226)

Not so Penelope. And yet, as we have seen, her waiting is not only patience and virtue. It contains both of Bergson's temporalities: time and duration, the chronology of the "clear" texture of her narrative of waiting and the vertigo of *achrony*. "Was it Ulysses?" asks Penelope upon awakening from her dream in Stevens' poem, "Or was it only the warmth of the sun / On her pillow? The thought kept beating in her like her heart . . . // It was Ulysses and it was not." The dual or duplicitous nature of Penelope's waiting – she wills it, she wills it not – is well expressed in her ambivalence towards the suitors:

> For three years now – and it will soon be four –
> she has been breaking the hearts of the Akhaians,
> holding out hope to all, and sending promises
> to each man privately – but thinking otherwise.
>
> (2.96–99)



The maid's discovery of Penelope's ruse is thus, as it were, the discovery of a psychological narrative woven with multiple threads. What happens within it becomes subject to rumor, suspicion, interpretation, doubt; it engenders different versions of Penelope's character and alternative legends of Odysseus' return. Among the numerous legends of Penelope – according to one, she succumbs in succession to each of her 129 suitors, another has her attempt suicide, another has Odysseus banish her, in yet another he kills her – in *The Odyssey* her waiting remains enigmatic, exhibiting the conscious and unconscious, the focused and diffuse, the day and night patterns that characterize her waiting – "She never / quite refused, nor went through with a marriage . . ." (24.142–143). If alternative legends of Penelope's waiting may exert less power upon us, it might be because they cannot wait, wanting hastily to foreclose the undecidable ambivalences allegorized in Penelope's weaving and unweaving.

Even as the loose threads of Penelope's nocturnal narrative of waiting are quickly reeled into the "tight" fabric of the heroic tradition, even as, in Benjamin's inversion, "the day unravels what the night was woven," the trace of the night remains. Penelope's weaving implies deeper complexities of artistic form, deeper word-shadows, than the "splendid shroud" might reveal. Its texture, as one of the commentators on Blanchot's *L'Attente l'oubli* puts it, has to "expose [itself] to the tumultuous, nocturnal excess, la *démesure*, and by withstanding this catastrophic immoderation, this devastating immediacy, bestow measure on it and on sheer boundlessness the limit of a form . . . ."[33]

The limit of a form might imply the metaphysical frame within which classical epics and tragedies, as Georg Lukács argues, run their course.[34] When Penelope returns from her suicidal nightmares of "cyclone winds" and "loathsome Furies" (20.86, 88), she returns to a time formalized in the ritual of her weaving. But while the daily weave of cloth bestows a measure on Penelope's nocturnal excess, and while the discovery of her ruse imposes a limit on the immoderation of her waiting, the texture of the shroud and the text of *The Odyssey* remain hermeneutically boundless. While Odysseus' return brings Penelope's waiting to an end, it does not interpret it. In our own reading, writing, and waiting, the text never ends. We unravel it again.

## THE END OF WAITING

And yet Penelope's waiting must come to an end. But perhaps rather than Odysseus bringing her waiting to an end, it is at the end of Penelope's waiting that he can return. "Thy firmness makes my circle just, / and makes me end where I begunne," declares, to that effect, the speaker in Donne's poem "A Valediction: Forbidding Mourning." As in Donne's poem, Penelope's and Odysseus' narratives are mutually causative and interdependent: "My lady," says Odysseus once they are reunited, "what ordeals have we not endured! Here, waiting / you had your grief, while my return dragged out . . ." (23.395–396).[35] Odysseus' protracted journey to Ithaca is mirrored in Penelope's waiting:

> the queen's cry reached Odysseus at his waking,
> so that he wondered, half asleep: it seemed
> she knew him, and stood near him! Then he woke
> and picked his bedding up. . . .
>
> (20.103–106)



Thus she, not he, appears to move the narrative on to its conclusion. As if to amplify this notion of mutual or reversed causality, Odysseus comes upon "a woman grinding flour / in the court nearby" whose activity – recalling the sand's flow through the hourglass – seems to parallel Penelope's measurements of time in her weaving. Like Penelope, the old woman is depicted as staunch and faithful: "all the rest, their bushels ground, were sleeping." To end a task is here not seen as a virtue; "one only, frail and slow, kept at it still" (20.118–120, 122–123). But the old woman's frailty and slowness indicate that the time of the end of waiting, and thus of the end of the narrative, is near. "[L]et this day be the last the suitors feed," declares the woman. "They've made me work my heart out till I drop, / grinding barley" (20.132–135).

In Penelope's weaving and unraveling, the proleptic and retrospective narrative patterns of *The Odyssey* – the dragging out of Odysseus' return, the grinding out of time – become visible, conceivable, possible. It is as if Homer were writing Odysseus' journey with a weaver's shuttle and every once in a while with a flour mill. During the night, he unravels his text so as not to come to the end of the story too soon, so as to threaten on repeated occasions – among the Lotus Eaters or the Sirens, by Circe's drugs or Calypso's spell – that Odysseus might altogether forget the return, or forget *The Odyssey* itself as Italo Calvino suggests.[36] Paul Ricoeur similarly reads *The Odyssey* as "a narrative that weaves together events and places, an epic that celebrates episodes and stops along the way as much as it does the indefinitely delayed return . . . ."[37] Like Homer, others explain, Penelope

> has a talent for procrastination, for unweaving what she has woven. And weaving is a common metaphor for song and narrative in the *Odyssey*. Because Penelope puts the suitors off by weaving her father-in-law's death shroud, there is something about her which is not only reminiscent of the Moirai, or Fates, who spin the threads of people's lives, but of the rhapsode, the poet, who reweaves the threads of traditional tales.[38]

Penelope's ruse only works if she weaves and unweaves, just as the writer, no less deceitfully, writes and revises, proffers and withdraws the promise of meaning and closure. Her unraveling can thus be seen as a revisionary, creative, or editorial activity in order to make possible new plot-lines, new textual patterns and pathways, new ways of home-coming, providing, as it were, other shores for Odysseus' narrative, other islands for his rescue, pleasure, and delay. *The Odyssey* itself seems to employ this revisionary process self-consciously in repeatedly making Odysseus, "the great master of invention" (19.194), retell his story so as to emphasize the story's gradual creative and revisionary evolution.

Literary texts, as the very texture of Penelope's weaving implies, allow the luxury of sustaining and delaying waiting when in ordinary lives such waiting would have long called for an expedient, pragmatic closure. Of this Clytemnaestra's story is exemplary: "Tyndáreus' daughter waited, too – how differently!" (24.224). And how differently do Penelope's suitors wait: "not one but swore to god to lie beside her" (18.267).

### THE END OF WAITING (CONTINUED)

Novels, as Benjamin has famously shown in "The Storyteller," are based on the principle of waiting; they are to answer the question "How do the characters make him [the reader] understand that death is already waiting for them . . . ."[39] The end of the novel, Benjamin suggests, can serve as a figurative death, which assigns, retrospectively, meaning to life. The same morbid significance is implicit in Laertes' shroud, whose unraveling not only keeps Odysseus away but Laertes alive. If waiting is thus the suspension of meaning, it is also the suspension of time and death and death's emblems: the beautiful object, the well wrought urn, the timeless text, the shroud: "let me finish my weaving before I marry," Penelope says to the suitors,

> or else my thread will have been spun in vain.
> It is a shroud I weave for Lord Laërtês
> when cold Death comes to lay him on his bier.
>
> (19.169–171)

As we return to narratives such as *The Odyssey,* we reopen the grave of Laertes; we spin again the thread of life. We return to a state of waiting, waiting again, or still waiting, knowing all the while how and when this waiting will come to an end. "In reading, one foresees; one waits," as Jean-Paul Sartre notes. "One foresees the end of the sentence, the following sentence, the next page. One waits for them to confirm or disappoint one's foresights."[40] And yet, although we wait for confirmation or disappointment, even as "[w]e project ourselves . . . past the End, so as to see the structure whole, a thing we cannot do from our spot of time in the middle," as Frank Kermode famously put it,[41] the wholeness of the structure, the completeness of the plot, even one's insights do not seem to provide a lasting satisfaction or indeed an answer to the question what it is that we wait for, or why we write or read. Although Penelope's decision to weave Laertes' shroud is an attempt to bestow on the sheer boundlessness of life the limit of a form (to echo Blanchot's words) – "let me finish my weaving before I marry" – her finishing of the shroud will be in vain, for with it her ruse will have failed,[42] unless it were to coincide with Odysseus' miraculous return. "And now, as matters stand at last," she confides to the disguised Odysseus, who has indeed returned, "I have no strength left to evade a marriage, / cannot find any further way . . ." (19.183–185). We are close to the end.

*The Odyssey*, as any story worth waiting for, must be complicated, delayed by multiple re-visionary processes, so that the desired end might still be possible.[43] But can any end, either mortal or miraculous, match the spinning of the thread of life or narrative? If this is a rhetorical question, it is so because the end seems ever deficient in proportion to time. No end can end time. Narratives are allegories of this paradox; they proffer endings that don't seem to be able to end the narrative. "[I]n art," writes Theodor Adorno, "the means are never completely absorbed by the end."[44] Once the end of a story is attained, the completed text must be unraveled anew – rethought, reread, rewritten, studied, argued about, as it is on numerous occasions in *The Odyssey* itself – so that we can wait again, so that the text can deceive us again, deceive us, that is, with the promise of an end worth waiting for. Even at the end when the royal pair had "mingled in love," they tell each other *The Odyssey* all over yet again: "hers of the siege her beauty stood at home" (23.337, 339), and his, considerably longer, including a censored version of his stay with Calypso. "She could not close her eyes till all was told" (23.347). But all will never be told, though precisely this is the deception of the story, that it would tell all. And that is why, as Peter Brooks observes, "fictional plots . . . impose an end which yet suggests a return, a new beginning: a rereading. Any narrative," he goes on to say, "wants at its end to refer us back to its middle, to the web of the text: to recapture us in its doomed energies."[45]

The attainment of the end of waiting, symbolically marked as it is in our tradition by death or by woman, would also signify the end of beauty. The role of the *femme fatale* – Calypso, Circe, Helen, or their later impersonations – may thus be to subvert this patriarchal objective. The *femme fatale*, who cannot be had, extends the time of waiting endlessly. She is to suggest that beauty cannot be had. It is not an end or an object. If it turns into an object, it is funereal; if a text turns into an object, it becomes a shroud. It is such objectification that Penelope delays in her unweaving. Finishing her cloth would turn her into a beautiful object to be exchanged for robes, necklaces, pendants, ear-drops. Having reached the end of the narrative, having finished her cloth, unaware of Odysseus' imminent return, Penelope sadly accepts this economy, "then mount[s] the stair again, / her maids behind, with treasure in their arms" (18.372–373).[46]

If "the created object always seems to us in a state of suspension,"[47] and if "one must wait for it," as Sartre suggests,[48] or, as Hans-Georg Gadamer puts it, if "the essence of our temporal experience of art is in learning how to tarry . . ."[49] it is to suggest that the experience of art is only deceptively initiated by the *work* of art, by art as a beautiful whole *object*. Beauty objectified is a dutiful shroud for a father-in-law. Beauty as object can only be had by denial of time. We recall Eurýmakhos' praise of Penelope's beauty where he denies her time of waiting. Either finished, tight, and clear as sun or moonlight, or masterful and majestic, objectified beauty will make us into suitors of beauty. It gives us the lie that there is an end to waiting.

If our own ordinary waiting seems unproductive or wasteful (to use adjectives that can be attributed to Penelope's suitors), literary texts assign it not only legitimacy and thus a deeper experience of time but also, as Penelope's waiting illustrates, the time to let events unfold, to assign them time so that they can end, if they have to, in their own time. While a bad story may reveal itself in the disappointment of having been simply a waiting for the expected end, a good story, on the other hand, may not provide what one may have been waiting for. Good stories insist on the potential of a narrative to make us wait forever, without making this waiting futile, and thus perhaps to intimate a waiting for which no expected end or object might suffice.

The story on which Odysseus embarks is thus only a temporary refuge from a waiting that will catch up with him again once he has returned, once this story is over. When he sets sail on his raft, Odysseus sails towards the illusory fulfillment of waiting. Upon waking from sleep after their first night together, Odysseus – "interminable adventurer" as Stevens calls him – announces to Penelope his imminent departure: "raids" to replenish his exhausted stores (23.403). In Dante's *Inferno*: "neither my fondness for my son nor pity / for my old father nor the love I owed / Penelope . . . was able to defeat in me the longing / I had to gain experience of the world" (26.94–98). In his poem "Ulysses," Tennyson has made Odysseus' restlessness proverbial: "I cannot rest from travel," complains Odysseus, "I am become a name; / For always roaming with a hungry heart / Much have I seen and known . . . ." The horizon which he scans in *The Odyssey* has here turned into a "margin [that] fades / Forever and forever when I move." Such waiting cannot be fulfilled. Each of the poems takes it up again.

# Lingering, Tarrying, Dwelling Upon: Elizabeth Bishop's "Poem"

# Five

> As I waited I heard a multitude of small sounds, and knew simultaneously that I had been hearing them all along . . .
>
> Elizabeth Bishop, "Time's Andromedas"

> One might almost say that truth itself depends on the tempo, the patience and perseverance of lingering with the particular.
>
> Theodor Adorno, *Minima Moralia*

## TARRYING

"In the experience of art," as the German philosopher Hans-Georg Gadamer writes in *The Relevance of the Beautiful*,

> . . . we must learn how to dwell upon the work in a specific way. When we dwell upon the work, there is no tedium involved, for the longer we allow ourselves, the more it displays its manifold riches to us. The essence of our temporal experience of art is in learning how to tarry in this way. And perhaps it is the only way that is granted to us finite beings to relate to what we call eternity.[1]

In the German original, Gadamer uses the word "*verweilen*," which is here translated as "to dwell upon" and "to tarry." The slightly archaic verb "to tarry" emphasizes the "specific" way of waiting implied in *verweilen*: "The *Weile* [the "while" in *verweilen*, tarrying] has this very special temporal structure," Gadamer explains in an interview, "a temporal structure of being moved, which one nevertheless cannot describe merely as duration, because duration means only further movement in a single direction. . . . [W]e learn from the work of art how to tarry."[2] Tarrying, moreover, does not involve tedium. It is a *tarrying* that might turn into the kind of *waiting* that Odysseus experiences on Calypso's island. Tarrying might turn into waiting when we give it a temporal direction (say, into the future) or an intention (to do something or to arrive somewhere). The less we wait impatiently, the more we tarry leisurely. The more we tarry, Gadamer suggests, the more the work of art reveals, because in tarrying we wait without object or purpose. In tarrying, we are receptive to let a work of art display its manifold riches to us. If we learn how to tarry in the finite temporality of the work of art, we intuit the infinite of which the work of art is a part.[3]

Tarrying, then, is a special way of waiting. It has affinities with the kind of non-directional, non-purposive waiting that French philosopher and activist Simone Weil advocates in her "Reflections on the Right Use of School Studies with a View to the Love of God."



> In every school exercise there is a special way of waiting upon truth, setting our hearts upon it, yet not allowing ourselves to go out in search of it. There is a way of giving our attention to the data of a problem in geometry without trying to find the solution or to the words of a Latin or Greek text without trying to arrive at the meaning, a way of waiting when we are writing, for the right word to come of itself at the end of our pen. . . .[4]

"The essence of our temporal experience of art is in learning how to tarry in this way," to repeat Gadamer's phrase. In this chapter, then, I shall ask how we practice a "special way of waiting" when we tarry, dwell, or linger – I shall use these words interchangeably – in a poem by Elizabeth Bishop. Does the work of art liberate us from waiting, in teaching us how to tarry?

### "POEM"

"I'm not interested in big-scale work as such. Something needn't be large to be good,"[5] Bishop declares in an interview. Even the furnishing of her house near Petrópolis in Brazil testifies to Bishop's preference for the small: "You will notice that the study turns its back on the view of the mountains – that's too distracting!" she explains. "But I have the intimate view to look at; the bamboo leaves are very close."[6] Bishop's "intimate view" is explicitly borne out in her poetry. In one of her poems, entitled "Poem," she ponders a small painting "about the size of an old style dollar bill."[7] In the minute size of this painting,[8] the moment and the infinite, the particular and the whole, form one continuity.

Thus, "The view is geared / (that is, the view's perspective)," Bishop writes in "The Monument," "so low there is no 'far away,' / and we are far away within the view."[9] Or thus in "Sandpiper," "The world is / minute and vast and clear."[10] The sandpiper who runs nimbly along the beach with his "focussed beak" is "a student of Blake," Bishop adds. When he stops and stares at the tiny spaces of sand between his toes – "where (no detail too small) the ocean drains / rapidly backwards and downwards" – the world is Blake's world in a grain of sand. It is minute and clear while retaining all the attributes of an incomprehensible vastness.

The world we experience in the "little painting" in Bishop's "Poem" is described as a rural scene in Nova Scotia. The speaker, poring over the specks and bits of color, the very "filaments of brush hairs," remembers in the barely recognizable white houses, trees, meadows, cows, and "half inch of blue sky," the small world of her childhood: "Heavens, I recognize the place, I know it!" she exclaims midway through the poem. The poem closes in its sixty-fourth line with a slight, quiet exuberance and the reverberation of an intimate loss. The "yet-to-be-dismantled" elms, as Helen Vendler has pointed out, are prophetic of the loss of the child's world.[11]

The exactitude and the almost devotional attention to the smallest detail –

> A specklike bird is flying to the left.
> Or is it a flyspeck looking like a bird?

– are Bishop's trademarks. In her poem "The Fish," her aesthetic is defined as "the tipping / of an object toward the light."[12] The painting in this poem is tipped towards the light three times. The landscape is described first in its painterly detail, then as a remembrance of an autobiographical past, and finally in a pastoral image.

The artist's brush strokes are minutely pondered to trace how they transform life into art. "[T]he gabled wooden houses" evoke – with unexpected accuracy – the memory of past emotions: "that awful shade of brown." The "thin church steeple / that gray-blue wisp" might on closer inspection be only a hair of the brush, while the "tiny cows" are painted with "two brush strokes each, but confidently cows." "Up closer" there is one single "wild iris, white and yellow, / fresh squiggled from the tube." But is the speck-like bird a bird or a flyspeck? Is the church steeple a hair? Is that there Miss Gillespie's house? How is one to tell one's life apart from the memory of it, from the painting of it, from the telling of it? ". . . life and the memory of it so compressed / they've turned into each other. Which is which?" the poet asks.

One must tarry, linger, draw closer (such are the implications) to disentangle this epistemological conundrum. What is revealed in the closer looking that lingering affords is the astounding, impenetrable gratuitousness of *all* phenomena:

> . . . how touching in detail
> – the little that we get for free,
> the little of our earthly trust. Not much.
> About the size of our abidance . . .

Here the word "size" returns from the first line, where it had been used to claim that this little painting "About the size of an old style dollar bill . . . has never earned any money in its life." Though art may not be distinguishable from life, it does seem distinguishable from money. It is not money. It earns nothing. The little painting is "Useless and free." In this it becomes analogous to our existence. For what is the value of existence? What does it amount to? "Not much." The word "little" puts into perspective but also into focus "our earthly trust," that is – our lives. It is little and yet it is what we "get for free." We are similar to art. In its phenomenology, Bishop seems to suggest, art is indistinguishable from life. "In the experience of art," Gadamer writes, "there is a plenitude of signification that cannot be solely attributed to its particular content or form, but that is representative of life as such."[13] In Bishop's "Poem," the plenitude of art is immeasurable, though ironically (typical for Bishop) inverted: it is "the little that we get for free." What we get for free is "About the size of our abidance," life as such, the essence of our temporal experience.

## OUR ABIDANCE

The painting, the size of an old style dollar bill, is as small and useless as our lives, as our endurance of and lingering in time. Our lingering before this painting, as before this poem, thus becomes an allegory of our mysterious, fortuitous "abidance," our being in time, time manifesting itself in our existence. If so, it would be no accident that this little painting, which has itself gradually become an allegory of time and human value, has the age of a human lifetime: "seventy years." The painting is "a minor family relic," as one might be oneself. Both art and life, if so unsentimentally observed in their surprising analogy and specificity, are "Useless and free." Life amounts to "Not much." It is "the little that we get for free." The allusions to Kant's aesthetic suggest that precisely in such suspension of ethical and practical purpose, the plenitude of essential life can be glimpsed, if only in miniature. We are not very visible, not very valuable either, nor masterpieces, yet what has made us – who amount to no more than an amateurish sketch done "in one breath," a speck, a squiggle of paint, a mere brush stroke, a hair – what has made us memorable are the minute particulars of a remembered life "compressed" and "cramped, / dim, on a piece of Bristol board." In this way, mysteriously, each thing comes into being. Or else all would have remained in the dark out of which the little painting has been taken and tipped towards the light.

This tipping towards the light, which both the painting and the poem accomplish – however modestly "dim" – has given occasion to a meditation on time, on the fleeting abidance of things. Things – but we as well – receive a brief afterlife, are remembered or acknowledged in the long, lingering look the poem allows: here then, briefly, is Uncle George, the painter of the little painting, who went back to England, "who was quite famous, an R.A. . . ." and who, we surmise, perished in the war. Then history fades into ellipses. *Pause.* "I never knew him," the poet muses. And yet, in "this place" which the painting and the poem memorialize, both she and Uncle George abide. In this sudden confluence of two lives, the poet's and her uncle's, her lingering substitutes for not-knowing; ". . . it is the only way that is granted to us finite beings to relate to what we call eternity."

The poem is about looking and lingering, the painter's and the poet's and ours, and in this looking and lingering, in this dwelling and tarrying, the vast becomes clear and minute, eternity momentarily contracts to instant, time to place – a world in a grain of sand, on a piece of Bristol board – in which the living and the dead abide, and in which the moment is the infinite. Although looking is not vision, Bishop protests, for vision "is / too serious a word," it is a looking nevertheless that entails the kind of self-transcendence that Bergson describes as "the intuition of our duration" which "puts us in contact with a whole continuity of durations which we should try to follow either downwardly or upwardly." When we think of duration "downward," we think of it as pure materiality; when we think of duration "upward," we think of it as intensity and eternity. "It would be," Bergson writes, "a living and consequently still moving eternity where our own duration would find itself like the vibrations of light. . . ."[14] Such intuitions of eternity cannot be conceptually initiated but must come about through what Weil calls "a special way of waiting." For

Bergson, this special way of waiting would be called "sympathy by which one is transported into the interior of an object in order to coincide with what there is unique and consequently inexpressible in it."[15]

I think this is precisely what Bishop means when she writes to Anne Stevenson: "What one seems to want in art, in experiencing it, is the same thing that is necessary for its creation, a self-forgetful, perfectly useless concentration."[16] In such useless concentration the passage of time is suddenly intensified:

We both knew this place,
apparently, this literal small backwater,
looked at it long enough to memorize it,
our years apart. How strange.

Strange, because such intensification of time happens on the minute scale of a Bristol board; strange because things hidden in places and vanishing in time suddenly appear in their unique and inexpressible ways. How are they? Strange, excerpted, small, particular. The droll specificity of things – the "arctics and overcoats, / lamps and magazines" in the waiting room – can suddenly be seen; the detail of our own brief abidance – our tarrying in time – becomes visible, gratuitously so, in the absence of larger justifications: "how live, how touching in detail / – the little that we get for free": our brief abidance, our tarrying, our life.

The poem ends with an image clear and pastoral, almost innocent:

the munching cows,
the iris, crisp and shivering, the water
still standing from spring freshets,
the yet-to-be dismantled elms, the geese.

There remains, like a small tear in this pastoral canvas, the thought of the elms to be dismantled, perhaps the thought of the geese who will fly away like Yeats's nine and fifty swans.

The small backwater, the cows, the iris, the elms, the geese, each visible detail of the painting exemplifies Bergson's observation that

> the delay of duration at instantaneity represents a certain hesitation or indetermination inherent in a certain part of things which holds all the rest suspended within it; in short, if there is a creative evolution, I can very well understand how the portion of time already unfolded may appear as juxtaposition in space and no longer as pure succession. . . ."[17]

Indeed, all things must make their *appearance* this way, as juxtapositions in space, as cramped on Bristol boards, as notes dwelled upon, as things, as hesitations; that *is* their manner of appearing just as this appears to be the only way that is granted to us finite beings to relate to what we call eternity. Even the note of the musical phrase appears as a juxtaposition in space, all appearances being minute, brief semblances of a delay in duration, a certain hesitation or indetermination of the vaster world contained therein. It is in such a delay of duration that the elms are "yet-to-be dismantled." In this lingering all the rest is suspended, all the rest is yet to come. It is in such a delay of duration that we experience the life that tarries within us. It is the little that we get for free.

## THE LINGERER'S EYES

What makes possible the discovery of the fragile pastoral image in the rush of time is the delay of duration, the moment of waiting – waiting *on* rather than waiting *for*, a special way of waiting, lingering rather than waiting. In this lingering things make their brief appearances: "the munching cows, / the iris, crisp and shivering, the water / still standing from spring freshets . . ." all come to be in what Theodor Adorno in a remarkable entry in his *Minima Moralia* has called "sabbath eyes," eyes that rest on their object. "The eyes that lose themselves to the one and only beauty are sabbath eyes. They save in their object something of the calm of its day of creation."[18] Sabbath eyes lose themselves not to a general or indiscriminate but "to the one and only beauty." The gaze of sabbath eyes is – in Bishop's poems as in Adorno's aesthetics – always won against the backdrop of larger, darker, historical necessities on the verge of breaking into the calm of such a gaze. Such a gaze, then, according to Adorno, has to sustain itself as an "obsession with the particular." "No gaze attains beauty that is not accompanied by indifference, indeed almost by contempt, for all that lies outside the object contemplated."[19]

The same "self-forgetful, perfectly useless concentration" (to repeat Bishop's words), the same obsession with the particular, the same indifference for all that lies outside characterizes the person who dwells upon the work of art. She is, to recall Sylviane Agacinski's words, the *flâneur* who "must be available to time, *to let time pass*, to spend it without keeping count, to know how to waste it. . . ."[20] But the notion of the lingerer as stroller also highlights the ethical accountability of lingering and looking. In her book *On Beauty and Being Just*, Elaine Scarry thus notes: "Beauty always takes place in the particular . . .";[21] it has thus incurred the charge that "by preoccupying our attention, [beauty] distracts attention from wrong social arrangements. It makes us inattentive, and therefore eventually indifferent, to the project of bringing about arrangements that are just."[22] How then is this charge addressed in Bishop's "Poem"? What are the moral obligations of the person who dwells on a painting, who lingers in a poem, who tarries, who wastes time?

In spite of the subtle but persistent intrusions of history into the contemplative scenery of this poem – even if it is here only a family history – the lingering gaze of the poet seems to serve precisely as the position from which consciousness of time, of loss, of history, and of death – in short, of duration in its material and metaphysical dimensions – is possible. Performed with sabbath eyes, Bishop's gaze – indeed our gaze as well – sees objects in their momentary hesitation in time, but the same eyes also cannot but see the same objects on the verge of their vanishing – downwards or upwards, into the material sweep of history or into metaphysical vibrations of light. The munching cows in their animal obliviousness, the crisp, shivering iris in its elegant elegiac fragility, the standing water in its indifferent solemnity, the elms in their doom, the migratory geese, all linger only because they have been seen in that "delay of duration," that "hesitation or indetermination," to recall Bergson's phrase, "inherent in a certain part of things . . ."[23] before they vanish again into the history, or into the eternity, from whose obliterating sweep they have momentarily been salvaged.

What we see of time are the casualties of time: the cows, the iris, the elms yet to be dismantled. The lingerer's sabbath eyes lift these particulars momentarily out of their evanescence, and in this lifting we "are transported into the interior of an object," feel its small, strange, excerpted particularity. How had it come to be here?

What the sabbath eyes see is "good" – for they see as if with the Creator's eyes at the beginning of time. "And God saw that it was good," we read at the end of each day in the Book of Genesis. Likewise, the sabbath eyes that linger on their object attend to the momentary completeness and justness and legitimacy of that object. They save it, momentarily, from the eternity into which the object is expelled outside of the poet's gaze. The aesthetic acknowledgment is, or reveals, the day of the creation of the object, that is to say, its singularity and particularity: the cows, the iris, the water, the elms, the geese. They are, to recall Bergson's terms, perceptions that "become 'perceptions' by their very isolation."[24] Then, some distance beyond the closure of this lingering gaze, one must imagine infinity, endless vibrations of light.

### THE LINGERING PARTICULAR

The sabbath eyes not only attend to the object in its relation to eternity, the sabbath eyes also survey the work of creation at the end of the Creator's week, on the threshold of historical time. The sabbath calm of the day of creation anticipates the storm of history. We cannot linger. "The particular is startled from its rapture," as Adorno notes. And yet, in this confrontation, the "just overall view" that seems to accuse the lingering gaze of irresponsibility or irrelevance is itself revealed as unjust. On the one hand, Adorno writes, "it is only infatuation, the unjust disregards for the claims of every existing thing, that does justice to what exists," but on the other hand the universal is unjust to the particular in that the universal is constituted by "exchangeability and substitution." To advance to the universal without the detour of the aesthetic would produce an empty concept of the universal: "what proceeds to judge, without having first been guilty of the injustice of contemplation, loses itself at last in emptiness."[25] While a poem such as Bishop's invites what I have called an exclusive, lingering gaze at the cost of a moral engagement with a collective universal, the same universal can constitute itself only in a disregard for the particularity of existence. In the universal – say, in the collective sweep of historical time – we do not see the cows munching, the crisp iris shivering, the still standing water, the elms to be dismantled, the geese. Nothing waits or lingers or hesitates in the sweep of collective time. The individual brush strokes, the paint squiggles, or the filaments of brushhair are invisible from that distance. Thus Adorno warns against the "just overall view" that such distance or such objectivity affords: "Indiscriminate kindness towards all carries the constant threat of indifference and remoteness to each. . . ."[26] Similarly, Scarry quotes Proust's observation that collective terms, such as "life" or "good books," erase "all beauty and happiness, which take place only in the particular."[27]

If it is from the larger, let us call it historical, perspective that things are judged for their relevance, function, or usefulness, and if such a judgment would always have to bear in mind its own injustice towards the particular, then the particular – like the lingering gaze – would not exist for its own sake but rather for the sake of assigning history a moral dimension. Adorno's dialectic between the particular and the universal is nothing if not passionately moral. He writes in *Aesthetic Theory*:

> Whereas in the real world all particulars are fungible, art protests against fungibility by holding up images of what reality itself might be like, if it were emancipated from the patterns of identification imposed on it. By the same token, art – the *imago* of the unexchangeable – verges on ideology because it makes us believe there are things in the world that are not for exchange. On behalf of the unexchangeable, art

must awaken a critical consciousness toward the world of exchangeable things.[28]

"The idleness of the flâneur is a demonstration against the division of labor," Benjamin notes in his *Arcades Project*.[29] The lingering of the poet is a demonstration against the multiplication of things. "Works of art," to quote again from *Aesthetic Theory*, "are plenipotentiaries of things beyond the mutilating sway of exchange, profit and false human needs."[30] Without art, history becomes monstrous; without art, the universal becomes totalitarian. The injustice of such collective terms as "life" or "history" resides in "exchangeability and substitution."

It is against such market values that the *flâneur* demonstrates, and it is against the pervasive currency of such values that the poet lingers. If their gestures strike us as childishly ineffectual, it is because they are. Like waiting, strolling and lingering are neither measurable nor marketable. We cannot linger. The sabbath will come to an end. Works of art are only plenipotentiaries, stewards not proprietors, of things beyond the mutilating sway of exchange. Bergson's lump of sugar will dissolve. Bishop's elms will be dismantled. Prufrock will drown. *But not yet*. Within the fragile sanctuary of the lingering gaze, the world must not yet be allowed to sever the connection to the particular in favor of the "just overall view." History must not yet be allowed to sever the connection to the individual in favor of the collective. It is in this temporality of "not yet" that we tarry.

Art, then, to use a phrase from Mikel Dufrenne's *Phenomenology of Aesthetic Experience*, is "something which surpasses history and does not have its truth in history. . . . If everything were caught up in the swirl of history, there would be no history at all."[31] The experience of the temporality of the work of art, recalling Gadamer's words, is acquired through tarrying. In tarrying, the subject is to have recourse to a defense of his or her minute abidance against its substitution and exchangeability. "But I felt: you are an I, / you are an *Elizabeth*," as we recall Elizabeth's exclamation . . .

> you are one of *them.*
> *Why* should you be one, too?
> I scarcely dared to look
> to see what it was I was.

The shy, sidelong glance of the little girl in this poem, who is about to discover the minuscule size of her abidance against a vast world at war outside, will become the lingering gaze of the poet. "[T]here is a special way of waiting upon the truth . . ."[32] as Simone Weil writes. "One might almost say that truth itself depends on the tempo, the patience and perseverance of lingering with the particular,"[33] Adorno explains. The size of our abidance, or the value of our existence, seems to be measurable in the patience and perseverance and lingering that "almost" constitute the truth. Adorno's restraint implied in the word "almost" avoids an aesthetic totalitarianism, and reserves the possibility for this lingering to be the allegorical truth. The same is also implied in the little word "*vielleicht*," which Gadamer interposes – like a hesitation, like a tarrying – in his claim that the experience of time in art "is *perhaps* the only way that is granted to us finite beings to relate to what we call eternity."

## THE STRANGE

"The eyes that lose themselves to the one and only beauty are sabbath eyes. They save in their object something of the calm of its day of creation." The gaze rests, tarries, lingers on its object, lifts it out of its obliterating contexts – eternity, history – into a privileged moment, and gives it something like a brief aesthetic justification. The object appears, momentarily, in its own right. Even if larger concerns necessarily "startle" the aesthetic gaze from its "rapture," as Adorno points out, the lingering gaze seems the only way to account for what he calls "the impenetrable."

The time of a work of art is a delay of duration, a certain hesitation, the tarrying of time, the detour of the sweep of historical time where the historical admits its injustice to the moment and to the particular thing. In historic discourses, objects appear in "abstracted correspondences," or in "exchangeability and substitution," or, we might say, in function and purpose. In the lingering gaze, objects appear in their impenetrable particularity. They are thus strange – like the little girl in "In the Waiting Room," or like the seal in "At the Fishhouses," whose sudden appearances are so singular that they seem veritably angelic, or like the moose, that "otherworldly" emissary from the impenetrable wood, in Bishop's poem of that title:

> A moose has come out of
> the impenetrable wood
> and stands there, looms, rather,
> in the middle of the road.[34]

Adorno notes in one of the last entries of *Minima Moralia* that "in existing without any purpose recognizable to men, animals hold out, as if for expression, their own names, utterly impossible to exchange. This makes them so beloved of children, their contemplation so blissful."[35] Moose, armadillos, dolphins, fish, mice, rabbits, crocodiles, cats, birds and dogs, a sandpiper, even a "Man-Moth," populate Bishop's poems, each of them enacting allegorically the strange particularity of art under the gaze of sabbath eyes. All things that are *not* strange are so because they are collective, synthetic correspondences, functions. Against such reduction of the particular to the universal, of the strange to the familiar, of the individual to the historical, Adorno repeatedly invokes a Schillerian conception of art as play, play as tarrying. "Play is their defense," he says of children:

> The little trucks travel nowhere and the tiny barrels on them are empty; yet they remain true to their destiny by not performing, not participating in the process of abstraction that levels down that destiny, but instead abide as allegories of what they are specifically for.[36]

"What we discover in history, and even thanks to it," Dufrenne points out, "is not altogether historical. We are persuaded of this by art itself. . . ."[37] What is not historical, in other words, tarries. What tarries is particular, incomparable, singular, strange, childish. Children ever tarry. We who are not strange, not childish, not incomparable are so only when we are similar and exchangeable, estranged from ourselves, un-emancipated from the schemata of imposed identification, hurrying – the antonym of tarrying – accomplished. But we are strange when we tarry. We are not strange when we hurry. The essence of our temporal experience of art is in learning how to tarry.

# Waiting for Death: Ferdinand Hodler's Paintings of Valentine Godé-Darel

# Six

It is only watching, waiting, attention.

Simone Weil, *Waiting for God*

Attention is waiting.

Maurice Blanchot, *The Infinite Conversation*

## ATTENTION

"The capacity to give one's attention to a sufferer, Simone Weil writes, "is a very rare and difficult thing; it is almost a miracle; it is a miracle."[1] Weil considers the kind of waiting that we perform in the presence of one who suffers as a subservience to nothing but waiting. Such waiting, for Weil, is not activity but substance – not an activity of the self but the substance of the self. It is the same substance submitted by one who waits faithfully for God and whose identity is nothing but his waiting. It is this kind of waiting one offers to a sufferer whose need, Weil notes, is not primarily that something gets done but that someone is there. The sufferer's need is above all the proximity of the other. With the sufferer one waits in Bergson's "profound time," which the French philosopher Emmanuel Levinas suggests is "interpreted as a relationship with the other and with God," and which Levinas paraphrases as

> *durée*, in which the spiritual is no longer reduced to an event of pure "knowledge," but would be the transcendence of a

relationship with someone, with an other: love, friendship, sympathy. A proximity that cannot be reduced to spatial categories or to modes of objectification and thematization.[2]

If waiting for death is performed in this inward realm of pure duration – time stripped of its illusory objectifications – then the waiting of the person who attends to the dying also eludes description. To wait with the dying is not a matter of length or efficacy but of proximity and sympathy. If bedpans have to be emptied, sheets changed, and drugs administered, such activities derive their quality entirely from the proximity and the sympathy of the person who performs them. What matters is that one give one's presence to the sufferer not as an activity but as the substance of waiting. "It is," Weil insists, "only watching, waiting, attention."[3]

Commenting on Weil's meditations on waiting, Maurice Blanchot explains that "Attention is waiting: not the effort, the tension, or the mobilization of knowledge around something with which one might concern oneself. Attention waits."[4] Such attention, Blanchot notes, is different from the "average, personal attention" which is merely a means to an end and which would be performed within the parameters of expectation and measurable time. The attention that is waiting, by contrast, is entirely open to the other. "It is not the self that is attentive in attention," Blanchot writes, "rather, with an extreme delicacy and through insensible, constant contacts, attention has always already detached me from myself, freeing me for the attention that I for an instant become."[5]

I am well aware that the Swiss painter Ferdinand Hodler's numerous sketches and paintings of his dying mistress, Valentine Godé-Darel, may document other motivations than saintly subservience to waiting. I will thus not attempt to trace

Hodler's motivations – whatever they were – but how the paintings, by way of their particular attention, reflect – and require of us – a proximity, a sympathy, a waiting that is wholly subservient to one who suffers, an attention that is waiting. That is hardly, I realize, a less speculative undertaking. The frankest way to ascertain such elusive objectives might be by asking how the paintings give their attention to the sufferer – a rare and difficult thing, according to Weil – how they *look* at her, and how we in turn *look* at Valentine Godé-Darel's ordeal through them. Are the paintings merely done as things that need to be done in the order of bedpans? Or are they done in the realm of *sympathy* that cannot be reduced to spatial categories or modes of objectification? Do the paintings heed Weil's imperative squarely to face the suffering of another and to ask the "indispensable" question: "What are you going through?" Do they "know how to look at him in a certain way?"[6] Let us look at some of Hodler's paintings of this series.



## ENDURANCE

Valentine Godé-Darel was dying of ovarian cancer from November 1914 until January 1915. Each of the paintings punctuates a time endlessly endured; each painting attends to Godé-Darel's suffering, from her initial expressions of hope and her gradual acknowledgment of the disease to her resignation and the long torment of dying. Hodler's cycle can be conceived as having its beginnings in two portraits, the first dated in the year 1909 (not shown here), where we view Godé-Darel with her head tossed back, her hat and dress implying a face one puts on in a portrait, altogether different from the solitary, intimate face we will witness in subsequent images.

I want to begin with a portrait painted just shortly before the onset of Godé-Darel's illness in 1912, where she appears in a typical frontal pose, in colors of red, tranquil yet vivacious, symmetrical, complete (Figure 6.1).

Her eyes calmly return the gaze of the painter or viewer. The red coloring intimates a fullness or completion, not just in aesthetic, but also, we feel, in emotional terms. The coloring in the next portrait is more complex, given the contrast between the gray background and Godé-Darel's tanned face; her greenish torso already announces – to one who reads these paintings as stations of waiting – colors that will explicitly mark her illness in subsequent paintings (Figure 6.2).

**Figure 6.1** Portrait of Valentine Godé-Darel, 1912

**Figure 6.2** Portrait of the ill Valentine Godé-Darel, 1914

The foreshadowing of her illness in this image is all the more poignant, since this is Hodler's first portrait of Godé-Darel after the birth of their daughter Paulette. In comparison with the previous portrait in red, here her head is slightly tilted and her eyes, set in shadows, seem tinged with a depth and melancholy at once questioning and resigned. While in the previous portrait her eyes rest on the viewer lightly, if intensely, here they rest heavily, as if they were to convey, silently, the burden of a premonition.

From now on, with the exception of a post-mortem portrait (Figure 6.3) – where her face seems serene, ethereal,

**Figure 6.3** Portrait of Valentine Godé-Darel (posthum.), 1915



emptied of the temporality of the other images – we will view Godé-Darel in successive stages of her illness, after two unsuccessful operations and experimental treatment with X-ray radiation, as a bedridden patient who increasingly must subject herself to the logic of her pathology.

In the image overleaf (Figure 6.4), her face has been consigned to the left of the frame while the two-thirds of the image on the right are dominated by the horizontality of her bed. "The dramatic expanse of space that comprises the actual center of the painting," as Sharon Hirsh has observed, "emphasizes the fact that, eventually, the void and

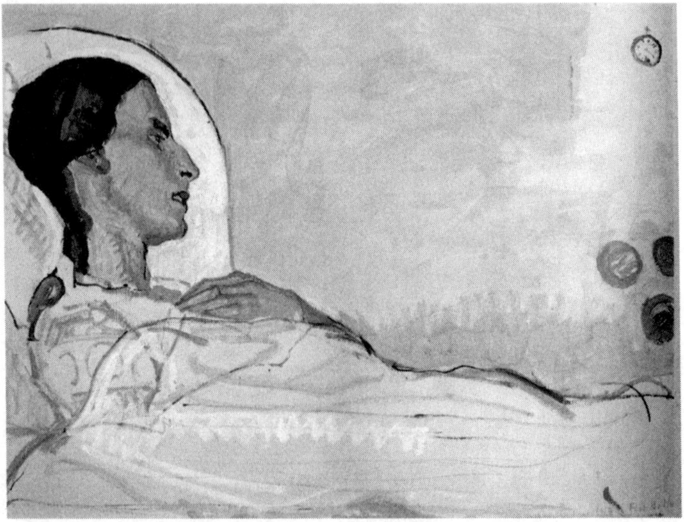

**Figure 6.4** Valentine Godé-Darel in her hospital bed, February 1914



the horizontality of death will overcome her."[7] While inflected with the symbolism of transience, the clock and the three roses at the foot of her bed seem incidental, redundant remainders, "modes of objectification and thematization" (to recall Levinas's words) of a time whose symbols and measurements no longer apply to Godé-Darel's "empty intimacy of time."[8] Her hand lies inertly on her upper body in a gesture of an inwardness that will gradually take hold of her and that will invoke the inwardness, I suggest, of what Levinas has called the face of the other. I will return to his concept of the face of the other in a moment.

The paintings now become a record of nothing but the impossibility of Godé-Darel fleeing from her pain. Death awaits her with a patience visible already in the very first paintings of the cycle. Hodler's artistic interpretations of these stages are rendered with decreasing idealization; the symbolic play with clock and roses falls utterly away when he portrays his beloved during her last two months, during which time each painting becomes a record of a rare and difficult attention: to the lineaments of Godé-Darel's suffering, to the weight of her head on her pillow, to the tautness of her skin over her cheekbones, to the gesture that a movement of the body unconsciously conveys. The sameness of Godé-Darel's position in several of these images permits emphasis on the subtle variations of her facial expression, allowing for our notice of the slightly differing depths of her breathing. The position of her body increasingly assumes the "severe horizontality"[9] of Hodler's depictions of Lake Geneva outside the window of Godé-Darel's room at a private clinic in Lausanne. In Hodler's paintings, during and after Godé-Darel's dying, the faint outlines of the French Alps across the lake, underneath a broad swath of sky, elegize in perhaps more universal

**Figure 6.5** Sunset over Lake Geneva, 1915

terms, what Hodler would have called the merging of soul and matter. "All things," Hodler writes as if paraphrasing Bergson's concept of the eventual reintegration of the particular in the whole, "have a tendency towards the horizontal, to spread out like water on the earth, even the mountains wear down with age until they lie flat like water."[10]

Godé-Darel's last attempt to return the gaze, and thus to be engaged in a communal acknowledgment of her suffering, appears in the painting where she seems to lift her head slightly towards the viewer, but her arms no longer support her (Figure 6.6).

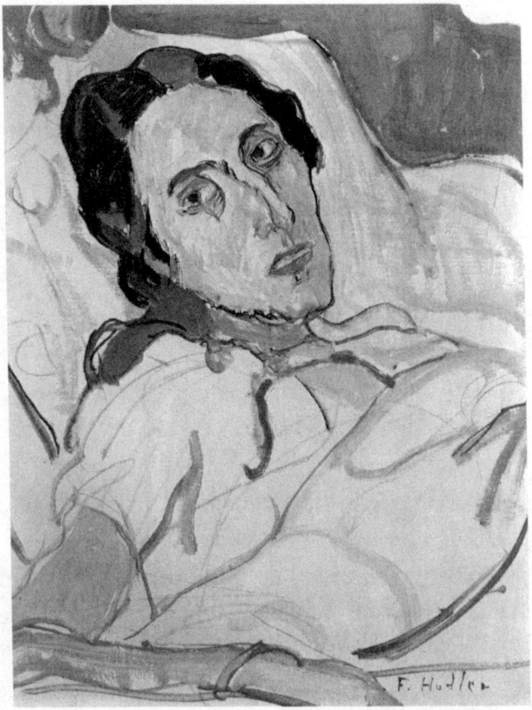


**Figure 6.6** The ill Valentine Godé-Darel, November 1914

The pale and at the same time excessively rose color of Godé-Darel's face and the expression of her eyes show the effort of her straining – also, perhaps, her fearful realization of her state. The rough lines of Hodler's brush around her eyes, nose, and jaw dramatize, not least by the stress – or is it haste? – with which they seem to have been applied, the swift progress of the illness. Godé-Darel's eyes seem silently to petition against her subjection to processes beyond her control – even perhaps her daily subjection to Hodler's painterly gaze. Neither time nor the timelessness of art will save her. Thus, the rough sketch in dull brown showing Godé-Darel on her side, her face expressing an unsharable suffering for which neither aesthetic idealization nor solidarity could offer remedy (Figure 6.7).

In many of the sketches Hodler drew during this time, Godé-Darel's face is already signed by death – beautifully – in the serene portrayal of her head, all in shades of green, as if to suggest, as Hodler would have wanted to imply, a reclaiming of her body by nature.

The horizontal lines of her bedding announce the horizontal lines of the earth and water outside her window, towards which she seems to be sinking (Figure 6.8). The calm of this scene does not recur in images where Godé-Darel lies on her back, with her head propped up, the stark outlines of her bones resembling the Alpine mountains and rocks Hodler painted throughout his life (Figure 6.9).

But, in spite of such reverberations in Hodler's earlier paintings, where vertical lines powerfully testify to the vitality of the natural world, Godé-Darel's sheets relentlessly flow towards the water outside her room, symbolizing that vast indifferent temporality of which she is a manifestation. Her mouth is open, as if each breath marked her endurance of the

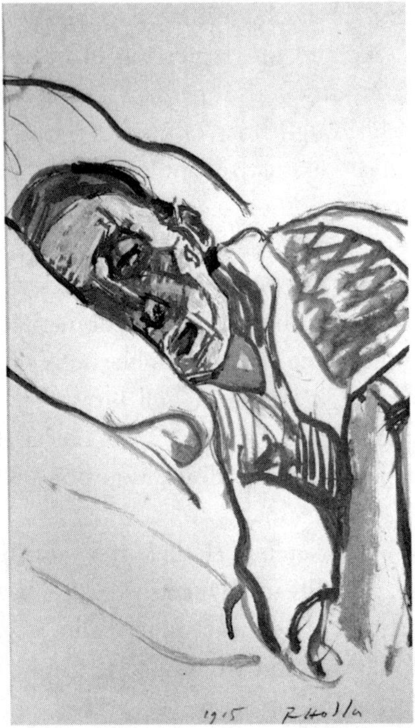


**Figure 6.7** The dying Valentine Godé-Darel, 1915



time in which mountains wear down – the time of suffering to death.

Each painting during this last month of her life not only documents Godé-Darel's endurance of her cancer but also exemplifies, in the sheer number of drawings and paintings – and in their intimate and urgent execution – that excessiveness, as Levinas calls it,[11] that the other's death demands. Each painting labors on and over this dying and manifests an "attention to the suffering of the other" that Levinas conceives as the only meaning that can be assigned to suffering.[12]

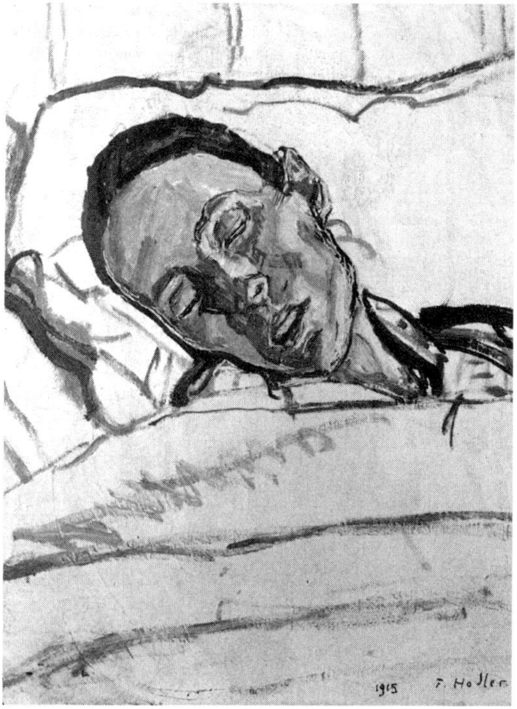


**Figure 6.8** The dying Valentine Godé-Darel, 1915



## THE FACE

At this point in this pictorial narrative of dying, Godé-Darel has withdrawn into a universe of suffering intimately her own. Before her is no longer her lover but her death. Now Godé-Darel's face appears in its most literal exemplification of what Levinas calls the naked face, the straightforward face, "which in [its] nakedness is an exposure unto death: nakedness, destitution, passivity, and pure vulnerability."[13] And thus the act of Hodler's exhibition of such intimacy must also admit the dangers of compulsive, intrusive, or voyeuristic motivations, as Elisabeth Bronfen has implied.[14] It is not a

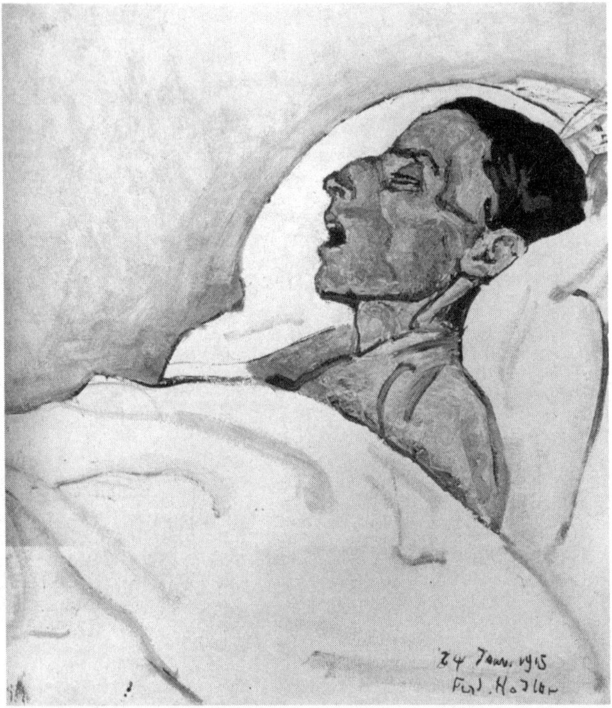


**Figure 6.9** The dying Valentine Godé-Darel, January 24, 1915



matter of *Mitleid*, as one of Hodler's commentators puts it, but of *Mitleiden*[15] – even as the near homophonic quality of these words implies the difficulties, perhaps the impossibility, of separating pity from empathy, or attention as means to an end from sacrificial, selfless attention. Weil's or Blanchot's concepts of an attention that is entirely detached from the self, "freeing me for the attention that I for an instant become"[16] would have to be reiterated in each painting. For, in order not to objectify the sufferer – which would be implied in sentimentality, pity, curiosity, aesthetic ideology – the painter must not re-present Godé-Darel as aesthetic object, but present himself – himself subsumed in his attention. Such presentation then, if I am following Weil's and Blanchot's implications, must be done through the painter's intuitions and instruments, by which the face remains intimate, incommensurable – "extra-ordinary" would be Levinas's word.[17]

Such a face in its innermost vulnerability cannot be grasped *thematically* or *conceptually*. It must therefore be painted *repeatedly*, every day from November 1914 until the end of January 1915. It is as if in this unceasing labor Hodler literalized Levinas's injunction that he who seizes his obligation "at the approach of [the other's] face, is never done with the neighbor."[18] Or it is as if, in this unceasing attention, Hodler exemplified, in painfully literal terms, Blanchot's injunction that attention-that-is-waiting "waits without precipitation, leaving empty what is empty and keeping our haste, our impatient desire, and, even more, our horror of emptiness from prematurely filling it in."[19] Each painting in this cycle, then, also literalizes Levinas's concept of the artwork's particular temporality. Each painting exemplifies "the imminence of an event that remains [in each painting] eternally suspended, an '*avenir*' that is always and only '*à venir*.' "[20]

Each painting, to say this differently, is structured not by a waiting with an object and a purpose, but by waiting *as such*. Each painting is to be conceived as an empty interval that, since it cannot be filled with a future, can only be filled with the proximity of one who waits with the person who suffers. The ethics of such waiting with the other is rendered by Levinas as an endless waiting:

> a responsibility with which one is never done, which does not cease with the neighbor's utmost extremity – despite the merciless and realistic expression of the doctor,

"condemning" a patient – even if the responsibility comes to nothing more at that time – as we powerlessly face the death of the other – than saying "here I am." . . .[21]

The announcement "here I am" does not imply a punctual, factual temporality, a present as instant that can be fulfilled, or be done with, in time. None of the paintings in the sequence acquires such formal or thematic finality; many of them seem, in fact, unfinished or sketched in haste, as if the lines of the pencil or the strokes of the brush were too final, too determinate to do justice to the random duration of suffering. Hodler's emphatic redrawing of pencil lines, his iterations and reiterations, sequences and variations of Godé-Darel's face and body trace her endurance of suffering, her movement through her illness, her illness moving through her, which no one line or brush stroke can arrest or objectify or turn into a beautiful thing. Each image reiterates the announcement "here I am," each line and image attends to a suffering with which one is never done.

And yet the concept of a series or movement also implies that such waiting and looking must come to an end. The painting dated January 24, 1915 (Figure 6.9 on page 100) is one of the last in which we see Godé-Darel barely alive. She dies the next day. In the painting of her dead body (Figure 6.10), her head is lowered to the level of land, water, and sky outside her window – that, as we have noted, had begun to form in the paintings, in the way her body flowed into the folds and creases of her gown and sheets.[22]

The evanescence of the moment, the imminence of an eternally suspended event that had engendered the other paintings, is gone. The vertical shoes seem to put a halt to the endurance of suffering. Here we see no longer Godé-Darel's

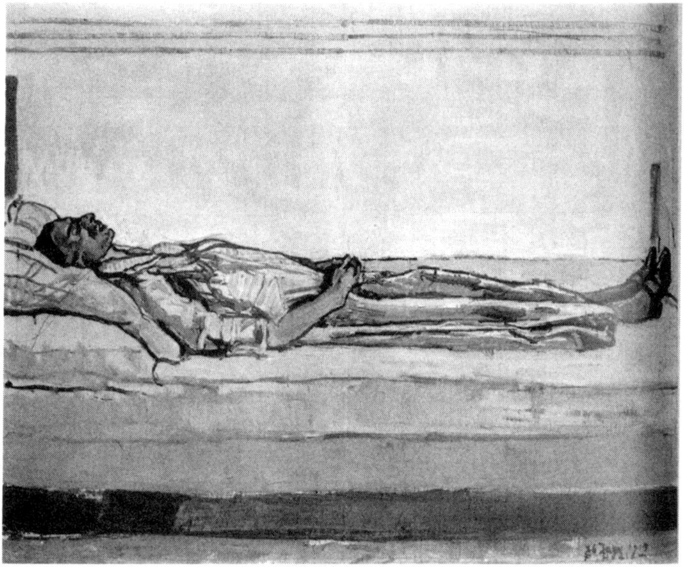

**Figure 6.10** The dead Valentine Godé-Darel, January 26, 1915

face but the material object of her body flowing with the duration of mountains "until they lie flat like water."[23]

## RESPONSIBILITIES OF WAITING

The face of the other constitutes the ground and reference point for Emmanuel Levinas's phenomenology of the other. From this face, in its "nakedness," in its "straightforwardness, before all verbal expression, in its mortality, from the depths of that weakness," Levinas intuits a fundamental moral imperative. From this face "an order [is] addressed to me, not to remain indifferent to that death, not to let the other die alone . . ."[24] but to attend to the other, to wait "not seeking anything," as Weil writes, "but ready to receive in its naked truth the object that is to penetrate it." Like the suffering other whose moan, cry, or groan utters what Levinas terms "the original call for aid, for curative help,"[25] the face of the other appeals with an analogous pre-conceptual, pre-linguistic voice, a voice anterior to philosophical conception or moral deliberation. "There arises, awakened by the silent and imperative language spoken by the face of the other . . . the solicitude of a responsibility I do not have to make up my mind to take on . . . ."[26] Hearing the moral imperative of the face of the other is to conceive a good that comes, as Levinas writes, from an immemorial past "without reference to an identity" or a presence.[27]

Levinas does not mean by "face" the actual countenance of the other but rather that which "in another concerns the I – concerns me – reminding me, from behind the countenance he puts on in his portrait, of his abandonment, his defenselessness and his mortality . . . ."[28] The face must thus "not be understood in a narrow way"; it is a metonymy for the human possibility "of signifying in its uniqueness, in the humility of its nakedness and mortality"; even "a bare arm sculpted by Rodin," Levinas adds, could accomplish such signifying.[29] Auguste Rodin's "bare arm" and Ferdinand Hodler's paintings and sketches of Valentine Godé-Darel during her mortal struggle with cancer have in common, I suggest, an expressivity and affective quality by which they are allegories of the face of the other.

But how can mere images – such as Hodler's cycle of paintings of Godé-Darel – make a moral claim upon us, as if images were perfectly transparent, moving us into the presence of one who suffers? That works of art should accomplish such transcendent signifying beyond their spatial finitude comes as a surprise if one reads Levinas's harsh critique of the image, chiefly in his early essay "Reality and Its Shadow." The opening statement of that essay at first appears to reflect

Levinas's own views: "An artwork," he declares, "prolongs, and goes beyond, common perception. What common perception trivializes and misses, an artwork apprehends in its irreducible essence. It thus coincides with metaphysical intuition. Where common language abdicates, a poem or a painting speaks." But Levinas will qualify such attributions of transcendent powers to art. Following Jean-Paul Sartre's suspicion about the self-referential opacity of art, Levinas similarly claims in "Reality and Its Shadow" that the opacity of art intervenes between us and our responsibility to the other, that art "is the very event of obscuring, a descent of the night, an invasion of shadow."[30] Since "an image marks a hold over us," it restricts our freedom to seize our responsibility in an open-ended relationship with the other. An image is a thing, according to Levinas, and to look at images is to be a thing among things, devoid of action or compassion.[31]

The image then, and this is the point of my digression about the opacity of the image, can keep us from attention-that-is-waiting, can make our waiting incidental, habitual, remote, repeatable, without sacrifice, even pleasurable. Rather than providing an occasion for an attention that is rare and difficult, an image can deflect and avoid such difficulty, an image can substitute for the attention to another. "[A]rt, essentially disengaged," Levinas writes in "Reality and Its Shadow," "constitutes, in a world of initiative and responsibility, a dimension of evasion." "There are times," he declares, "when one can be ashamed of it, as of feasting during a plague."[32]

Levinas's warnings against art's seductive substitutions for real engagement and proximity render problematic not only Hodler's daily markings and delineations of Godé-Darel's slow dying, but also our own coming face to face with this astoundingly deliberate pictorial documentary of suffering. If the question is – and of course it is – how we should behave in the face of another's suffering, Levinas answers throughout his work: by not remaining indifferent, by not letting the other die alone, by saying, "here I am." And yet, we might insist, how exactly can an image, a bare arm sculpted by Rodin, or Hodler's cycle of paintings – how can they overcome their opacity, their absorption in the thing, their own spatial finitude? How can paintings in their flat, silent markings utter the sufferer's call for aid, for curative help? "How," asks Levinas analogously, "is the vision of the face no longer vision, but hearing and speech?"[33]

Just as the face of the other, as Levinas writes, "does not have the coercive power of the visible," Hodler's paintings, I claim, do not derive their qualities from what Levinas regards as the reductive intentions of "re-presentation" or from "the objectivity of the visible." The "power of the visible" is coercive because it preempts "a responsibility anterior to . . . logical deliberation"[34] as we exercise it in what Mieke Bal has called the rhetorical gaze or in what Bronfen describes as rhetorical violence.[35] The rhetorical gaze is the average attention that is merely the means to an end. The rhetorical gaze does not wait; it has always already come to the end of waiting and seen what it anticipated.

The painting opposite (Figure 6.11) might exemplify, by contrast, the non-rhetorical, non-coercive characteristics of artistic presentation. The calm of the composition, the exclusive focus on the face, the reflection of the light on its contours, the deep shadowing of the middle of the face, the asymmetrically closed eyelids, all convey the extraordinary of the face, whose signifying seems no longer limited to, or by, the visible.

**Figure 6.11** The dying Valentine Godé-Darel, 1915

While representation, according to Levinas, "ceaselessly covers over the nakedness of the face, giving it content and composure in a world,"[36] making it the face one puts on in a portrait, Hodler's artistic style, I claim, ruptures that ceaseless covering over, retaining the extra-ordinary of the face. Extra-ordinary, external to thematic content and social composure, the alterity of Godé-Darel's face is infinitely other, intimately individual. Hodler's relentless attention to the smallest changes of Godé-Darel's face announces an absolute otherness, an incomparable singularity. Compelled by signifying powers such as Levinas grants to Rodin's arm or that Bergson grants to poetic language, Hodler's paintings of Godé-Darel's face thus awaken a response – indeed a responsibility – "anterior to . . . logical deliberation."[37] If art is "an activity that gives things a face," as Levinas proposes,[38] the mutually exclusive alternatives of Bronfen's questions – "... do we ask ourselves, are these paintings skilfully done? Or do we ask ourselves, does the woman suffer? Do we see the woman's pain? Can we really see this pain?"[39] – would have collapsed in the transcendent qualities of the face that the paintings present. The power of Hodler's paintings, I suggest, resides in that we do not ask ourselves if the paintings are skillfully done *or* if the woman suffers. To view the paintings in such mutually exclusive terms would be to view them in a temporality that abstracts, fragments, and separates, rather than in the temporality of *durée* that allows us to enter into "a proximity that cannot be reduced to spatial categories or to modes of objectification and thematization."[40] It is, in short, precisely because of the paintings' particular aesthetic that the aesthetic does not intervene between us and the woman who suffers; it is because of the paintings' visual qualities that the visual does not blind us to the woman's pain.

What I have been trying to convey in what I hope are not illegitimately complicated ways is how looking at these images necessitates our proximity, our watching, waiting, and attention whereby the images will disclose – despite their spatial finitude, despite their material opacity – the endurance of one who suffers. When, from December 1914 until her death at the end of January 1915, Godé-Darel does not return the painter's gaze, when her eyes remain closed, when her face appears like that of one drowning in her bed, when she is not facing us, her face regards us in its most defenseless straightforwardness. What we see before us – to bring these considerations back to the subject of waiting – is the immanence of a death endlessly delayed in suffering. "This future of death in the present of love," writes Levinas, "is probably one of the original secrets of temporality itself and beyond all metaphor."[41] If Hodler's paintings keep a secret, the secret does not reveal itself in concept or in understanding. Bronfen's questions remain undecidable, perhaps irrelevant. The secret of temporality is kept in that it must be endured. Such endurance constitutes the incommensurability of the face, whose secret, whose intimacy of time, can be sympathetically intuited, perhaps in the painter's, perhaps in the viewer's, attention that is waiting. "Here I am," is what we must say.

Waiting and Hoping: Raymond Carver's "A Small, Good Thing"

# Seven

We've been waiting with him until he died.

Raymond Carver, "A Small, Good Thing"

. . . wait without hope
For hope would be hope in the wrong thing.

T.S. Eliot, *Four Quartets*

In his brief meditation "Poseidon and Company" Raymond Carver ponders thought and felt time. A boy lies languidly at the ocean's edge overhearing far off the voices of the other boys. The boy drifts into daydreaming:

> He lay again on his stomach and turned his face a little to one side, waiting. On his back the sun slipped away and a chill broke over his legs and shoulders. Tonight he would lie wrapped in his cover and remember these few minutes of felt time, day fading. It was different than standing in Naiad's cave up in the hills, someone holding his hand under the water that trickled steadily out of the crack in the rock. It had been dripping for no one knows how long, they said. Different too than wading in the surf up to his knees, feeling the strange pull. That was time too, but not the same . . . . every afternoon he lay on his stomach up over the sea and waited for the change, the prickly passage of time across his back.[1]

Time and duration: the trickle of time in Naiad's cave, the rhythm of time in the surf, but the difference of another time whose passage – if only for a few minutes – is felt, not known, and during which time, as Carver implies, one is fundamentally separate from others. " 'There you are!' " The boy suddenly hears his sister's voice, " 'I had to walk all this way for you! Why didn't you come home?' "[2]

### THE WAITING ROOM

Some of the implications of this early piece reverberate in Carver's later story "A Small, Good Thing," where a little boy is hit by a car on his eighth birthday while walking home from school. Like Scotty, who lies in a deepening coma, the little boy in Carver's early fragment drifts in his own time and cannot hear his sister calling.

"A Small, Good Thing" tells of the parents' waiting for their son to wake up. As the father drives home from the hospital to take a bath, his interior monologue of Scotty's accident traverses the past perfect, the past, and the future tenses in order to retrace an order of events, and to align them in a sequence that would predict his son's recovery: "Scotty had been hit . . . and was in the hospital . . . he was going to be all right."[3] When Howard arrives at home, the telephone rings: Scotty's birthday cake had not been picked up. The baker calls repeatedly throughout the story. The cake, once symbol of a celebratory marking of time, thus becomes an ironic reminder of human powerlessness over time. Scotty *should have been* eight years old, the birthday cake *should have been* picked up. But the eight candles and the outstanding debt for the cake mark a time wholly other than the child's. Time, as the unclaimed birthday cake signifies, runs its course indifferent to expectation, indifferent to the rituals and celebrations by which we harness time to human desire.

When Howard calls the hospital, "the child's condition remained the same; he was still sleeping and nothing had changed there."[4] Despite everyone's attempts to alter the course of the boy's mortal destiny, the time in which nothing happens from here on determines the plot of this story. "They waited all day, but still the boy did not wake up."[5]

The child has slipped into a time that passes beyond the powers of clinical prediction, beyond expectation, beyond meaning or measurement. The child is, to employ Maurice Blanchot's phrase, "time indefinitely endured."[6] The unclaimed birthday cake is the representative missing sign that would have punctuated, arrested, interpreted this mere duration to which the child has been reduced.

The parents wait. They wait in a "liminal space," as Laura Tanner has characterized hospital waiting rooms, through which "we pass to somewhere else."[7] " 'Go home for a while, and then come back . . .' " says the husband,[8] as if one could leave this waiting and then return. But waiting, as the story will tell, is not to be passed through. The waiting room literalizes what Bergson would call a clear, precise but impersonal temporal consciousness,[9] not real time but the illusion of time. Thus the doctor's assurance, "It's just a question of a little more time now,"[10] rings hollow, for these are vain projections. And the numerous other temporal announcements only indicate the impatience and impotence of desire cast into the frame of hours and minutes:

> "Doctor will be in again shortly";
> "Dr. Francis will be here in a few minutes . . .";
> "We'll know some more in a couple of hours . . .";
> "We'll know more when he wakes up";
> "I was gone for exactly an hour and fifteen minutes";
> "Maybe I *will* go home for a few minutes";
> "I won't be gone long."[11]

If these announcements and predictions attempt to control life by controlling time, time, as the narrative progresses, simply runs its course: the parents wait, the doctors come and go. "In an hour, another doctor came in. He said his name was Parsons from Radiology. He had a bushy moustache. He was wearing loafers, a Western shirt, and a pair of jeans."[12] The gratuitous listing of the details of the doctor's attire conveys the typical visual fixation experienced by the person who waits, whose strained concentration on an invisible future transfers to the visible details of her present.

Numerous entrances and exits by the parents, doctors, nurses, lab technicians, and orderlies punctuate the boy's slipping into an intimate, immeasurable time. All of them perform in their activities the temporal increments by which the child's otherworldliness, they hope, could be reeled back into their world:

> He moved to the side of the bed and took the boy's pulse. He peeled back one eyelid and then the other. Howard and Ann stood beside the doctor and watched. Then the doctor turned back the covers and listened to the boy's heart and lungs with his stethoscope. He pressed his fingers here and there on the abdomen. When he was finished, he went to the end of the bed and studied the chart. He noted the time, scribbled something on the chart . . . .[13]

The laconic brevity of the sentences and the detailed listing of the doctor's examination relieve the parents, for a time, from their worry about the development of the boy's condition. The measured, timed, and sequential succession of Carver's sentences, as of the doctor's actions, simulates a world of order and predictability. Likewise, the doctor's appearance – "handsome, big-shouldered . . . with a tanned face" – and his "three-piece blue suit, . . . striped tie, and ivory cuff links" are welcome visual distractions – messages as if from a world impervious to death – in the midst of deepening dread. By contrast with such temporary markers of reassurance, the doctor's subsequent interpretation of the boy's condition reveals, however, his profounder sense of uncertainty and the disjuncture between their and the boy's temporal realms: " 'He's all right . . . . he could be better . . . . I wish he'd wake up. He should wake up pretty soon.' "[14] Again, as in the father's drive home from the hospital, the permutations of the temporal modes of the verb "to be" – he is, he could be, he should be – indicate the doctor's difficulties in locating the child's being.

His coma has removed the child into a temporal realm that no one can enter. The expectation that Scotty will awaken from his coma, the confidence of the doctors, the anticipation of the parents, all take place in that authoritative temporality that is measured by clocks. But as the boy's symptoms remain unchanged, the parents slowly move into a waiting whose end is no longer defined by hours and minutes, or by prognosis and expectation.



"But he's out of any real danger?" Howard said. "You said before he's not in a coma. You wouldn't call this a coma, then – would you, doctor?" Howard waited. He looked at the doctor.

"No, I don't want to call it a coma," the doctor said and glanced over at the boy once more. "He's just in a very deep sleep. It's a restorative measure the body is taking on its own. He's out of any real danger, I'd say that for certain, yes. But we'll know more when he wakes up and the other tests are in," the doctor said.

"It's a coma," Ann said. "Of sorts."

"It's not a coma yet, not exactly," the doctor said. "I wouldn't want to call it a coma. Not yet, anyway."[15]

The doctor's initial evasions and denials cannot conceal his forebodings. Ann's sudden rejoinder, "It's a coma," hastily but only partially withdrawn, permits the doctor's own admission, equally unintentional, that what all are waiting for might precisely be that which cannot be waited for. If the doctors' assurances were once offered entirely within the dimensions of measurable time – it being just a matter of time until the child would wake up – his qualifications, "Not yet," "It's not a coma yet," deny closure. Now waiting is open, potentially unending, no longer to be passed through.

The suffering of the child in a coma is no longer what Blanchot has described as "a measured suffering" that can be "brought back into our grasp and assumed, recaptured and even comprehended in the patience we become in the face of it." The boy's coma has removed him into a suffering that has lost this measure: "Suffering is suffering," writes Blanchot,

> when one can no longer suffer it, and when, because of this non-power, one cannot cease suffering it . . . . There, the present is without end, separated from every other present by an inexhaustible and empty infinite, the very infinite of suffering, and thus dispossessed of any future . . . . Suffering has simply lost its hold on time, and has made us lose time.[16]

Blanchot's comments on this immeasurable suffering seem not only pertinent to the nature of a coma, endured as it must be in an empty infinite, but also to Scotty's parents, who must begin an unceasing suffering in their realization of the gravity of their child's condition. As their child drifts towards death, Ann and Howard are like their child ". . . delivered over to another time," as Blanchot calls it, to time as other, as absence and neutrality; precisely to a time that can no longer redeem [*racheter*] us, that constitutes no recourse. A time without event, without project, without possibility . . . a time neither abiding nor granting the simplicity of a dwelling place [*demeure*].[17]

When Ann and Howard stand gazing out into the night, down at the parking lot far below their window, the dwelling place of time, once shaped by expectations and institutional assurances, now expands to infinity. Waiting endured in such time is not a matter of time. Such waiting cannot be accomplished in the doctor's projections that " 'We'll know some more in a couple of hours . . .' ";[18] nor does waiting in that other time have the shape and closure of " 'exactly an hour and fifteen minutes' "[19] that Howard claims he was gone before he returned to his son's bed. These measurements ought to shelter us from that immeasurable other time that we enter when references to hours and minutes, predictions and diagnoses, no longer measure up.



### THE PARKING LOT

When Ann intuits her husband's need "to be by himself for a while, not have to talk or share his worry for a time,"[20] he descends to the empty, infinite plane of duration, a time without event, without project, without possibility, a time neither abiding nor granting the simplicity of hours and minutes, a time where one is separate, unreachable by others, like the boy in Carver's fragment who does not hear his sister's voice calling him home. And yet, paradoxically, it is in her intuition of her brother's separateness that the sister knows her brother most closely, just as it is in her intuition of Howard's need for privacy that Ann moves closer to him. The paradox of closeness, or intimacy, then, is in the suggestion of a proximity that can only be attained without space and measure and limits, as indeed such intimacy is also the mark of extreme suffering, which is likewise without space and measure and limits as it is endured in the most intimate proximity. Since intimacy, then, seems attainable only in duration, not in that functional time that requires and permits our self-externalization, duration, as Levinas (paraphrasing Bergson) points out, "is experienced by a descent into self."[21]

The time that is here allowed for Howard's descent into his self commences a waiting simply to be endured. If Ann and Howard will have to wait forever, they will have to wait in that paradoxical time that Blanchot designates as the unbearable present: "a present without end and yet impossible as a present."[22] Ann and Howard must revise their waiting to hoping; they must endure an undefined, unquantifiable waiting, a waiting without sign or image of future things to pass. Such waiting, such hope, in Levinas's words, "is projected nontemporally into the domain of pure nothingness."[23] Hope is purely qualitative, an inward intimate waiting, an intensity rather than an extensity, not determined by prediction and anticipation.

Like despair, from which it is often only thinly divided, hope is endured, felt rather than known in the depths of self, there where Howard is "by himself for a while, not [having] to talk or share his worry for a time." The temporal indicators "for a while" and "for a time" mentioned in Howard's descent into himself refer to a time that runs its course eminently outside of him and without him, like the drip of water in Naiad's cave, like the ebb and flow of the ocean tides. During his brief absence from the official coordinates of the time in which doctors come and go, in which one waits *for something*, Howard is enduring; he becomes the time that passes.

It may be in such radical existential reduction that Howard is intimately aligned with Scotty's comatose drifting; both are open unto infinite lack, both share, as Blanchot writes in a related context, "the empty intimacy of time."[24] If Blanchot calls such waiting "affliction", we may call hope an affliction. One *has* expectations but one *suffers* hope. "Through affliction," writes Blanchot,

> we endure "pure" time, time without event, without project and without possibility; a kind of empty perpetuity that must be borne infinitely . . . . Deprived of ourselves, deprived of the I upon which we naturally lean, deprived of the world that in normal times exists in our place and disburdens us of ourselves, we are time, indefinitely endured.[25]

Such afflicted waiting comes about through the renunciation of the superficial consciousness of time. " 'Maybe,' " says Ann, " 'if I'm not just sitting right here watching him every second, he'll wake up and be all right. You know? Maybe he'll wake up if I'm not here.' "[26] Withdrawing her vigilance, she thinks, might call the child forth; but rather it calls her to the child, connects her more intimately with her child, as if in such renunciation of time and consciousness she might intuit his being outside of consciousness, in that realm where nothing needs to be waited for, where waiting opens unto the domain of pure nothingness. In their most private moments, thus, as when "Ann walked to the window and looked out at the parking lot,"[27] Howard and Ann enter the most intimate dimensions of waiting, a waiting momentarily released from its strained intentionality, calibrated to their child's drifting, marked by the loss of measurable time, sustained by their suffering of hope.

This kind of waiting can set in, as Hans-Jost Frey writes,

> when one has waited for something so long, without seeing any signs of imminent fulfillment, that the object of expectation gradually begins to fade, and yet one does not stop waiting. The state of unfulfillment lasts unchanged, but the hope of putting an end to it has been imperceptibly eroded and the waiting has become empty, mere opening onto infinite lack.[28]

In Carver's blandly ordinary world, this waiting in the depths of self, beyond the dimensions of time and beyond what can be waited for, is endured in the gaze out of the hospital window onto a parking lot. "It was night, and cars were driving into and out of the parking lot with their lights on."[29] The ordinariness of the scene and the casualness of Ann's gaze suggest that her waiting will become habitual. The death of her son opens her waiting unto infinite lack, making it interminable.

The night scene outside the window reveals the detached, indifferent, immeasurable superfluity of existence. In the cars "driving into and out of the parking lot," life is generic, mindlessly in motion, markedly unlike the purposeful comings and goings of doctors, nurses, and orderlies. Eventually, Ann and Howard too will join this fluid, blind movement of all things when they leave the hospital after their son's death. From Ann's distant perspective at the window, the cars appear anonymous, sliding noiselessly in and out of the parking lot, performing a silent procession of lights, a ritual of endless, anonymous comings and goings. Ann looks into a realm devoid of the human dimensions of time. The cars below her window perform the fluid, circular movements of a Schopenhauerian time as blind will, in which nothing happens or changes, in which cars will ever enter parking lots of hospitals, a time older and other than the time of the doctors' predictions or the parents' expectations. It is in this encounter with what a phenomenologist would call a plane of emptiness, and which emptiness also implies the despair thinly held back, that Ann "knew in her heart that they were into something now, something hard."[30]

Gazing out of the hospital window, Ann

> saw a big car stop in front of the hospital and someone, a woman in a long coat, get into the car. She wished she were that woman and somebody, anybody, was driving her away from here to somewhere else, a place where she would find Scotty waiting for her . . . .[31]

The stopping car momentarily interrupts and humanizes the anonymity of the night scene outside the hospital. Ann's inversion of her and her son's roles projects each of them into a time where all waiting would be fulfilled. She has momentarily saved him from his aimless drifting in the vast fluid motions of duration and assigned him a firm destination where he waits for her. She has imaginatively seized the pure duration by which he was carried away in order to emplot his enduring, to give it meaning and measure, in order to make his drifting come to an end.

Driven by "somebody, anybody . . . somewhere else, a place where she would find Scotty," she has undertaken a mythic passage to an otherworldly realm. Her desire is for a closure of pre-linguistic, pre-temporal dimensions, to collapse her and her son's times into a time not yet bifurcated into mother and child, life and death, a time where no one would have to wait for the other, where he would "let her gather him into her arms,"[32] as if he were profoundly reunited with his mother, as if he were unborn in his mother's womb. The time of such desire is a time before time; it is the suspension of time.

### THE CATHEDRAL

In the opening paragraphs of the story where Ann enters the bakery to order the birthday cake, Carver's sparse descriptions of the baker's uncared-for appearance and lethargic movements convey a person suffering from chronic depression: "He let her take her time. He'd just come to work and he'd be there all night, baking, and he was in no real hurry."[33] In the tedium of his work, the baker will later tell Ann and Howard, he endures time as endless, repetitive; for to be childless, he says, is "To repeat the days with the ovens endlessly full and endlessly empty."[34] For to be childless, he implies, is to live in the indifference and superfluity of mere duration, a time rendered blind and futile by "hundreds, no thousands" of birthdays and cakes, a time without markers or meaning.

It is in the context of depletion and loss, of childlessness and the death of a child, that the ending of the story must itself appear as the unexpected end, that which could not have been waited for. After the death of their child, Ann and Howard, having first driven home, then driven to the bakery to confront the baker about his phone calls, find themselves unexpectedly sharing a meal with the baker under the "high pale cast of light in the windows."[35] In a story of so much waiting, such an ending – as perhaps in any good story – could not have been waited for other than in that radical openness that constitutes that deeper, hopeful waiting that one attains after having waited in vain. The unexpected, transformative qualities of Carver's ending all seem suggested in Simone Weil's notion of faithful waiting, which she illustrates through a paraphrase of the biblical parable of the absent landlord: faithful waiting, she writes, is performed "while the master is absent"; upon his return the faithful is

> ready to open the door to him as soon as he knocks. The master will then make his slave sit down and himself serve him with meat. Only this waiting, this attention, can move the master to treat his slave with such amazing tenderness.[36]

These mystical, transformative, and metaphoric qualities of the story's ending – though not played out in the same roles or parts – may have been initiated when Ann walked past the black family back in the hospital who were "in the same kind of waiting she was in."[37] Ann is tempted to ask the older woman whose lips were "moving silently" to share her words. But the allusions to prayer – the passage is predictably deleted in the earlier draft edited by Gordon Lish – suggest metaphysical realms that will remain only implicit – but powerfully so – and thus come to bear in the story's last scene, where the parents and the baker come together on a plane altogether removed from the world of time: "They talked on into the early morning, the high pale cast of light in the windows, and they did not think of leaving."[38]

When Howard, back in the hospital room, gets up and goes "over to stand beside her at the window,"[39] the redemptive closure in the bakery seems yet inconceivable. But Howard's and Ann's descent into a waiting beyond the certainties of expectation and beyond their fear has here begun. He and his wife have descended into an intimate, infinite realm of hope in which each is revealed to the other despite and because they are in their innermost, separate selves: "They both stared out at the parking lot. They didn't say anything. But they seemed to feel each other's insides now, as though the worry had made them transparent in a perfectly natural way." Then, predictably, "The door opened and Dr. Francis came in. He was wearing a different suit . . . ."[40] But the jolt in the movement of the narrative from a deeper to a surface time, from inside to outside, cannot dispel Howard's and Ann's encounter with an intimate, inward sense of a mutuality that is attained in the shared endurance of hope.

The bakery, whose "high pale cast of light in the windows" recalls Carver's story "Cathedral," extends this mutuality in which the plane of emptiness has suddenly been populated, in which the infinite lack is suddenly filled – not by what was expected, or waited for, but by mutual revelations of inwardness. Here in the bakery, then, as symbol of such plenitude, the empty planes of duration are gathered up, structured, and humanized by an impromptu celebration. Scotty's birthday cake is replaced by a symbolically wholesome bread, "heavy" and "rich"; the baker's sudden elated deliberateness lifts out of oblivion one of those "hundreds, no thousands" of unclaimed celebrations in which he had lived in his own plane of emptiness and mourned his own lack; his serving of cinnamon rolls, "the icing still running," now arrests the futile repetitions of a time in which "ovens are endlessly full and endlessly empty." Carver's story ends at the felicitous moment of an unwaited-for, unaccountable plenitude. Once the baker has served Ann and Howard their rolls and butter, "[h]e waited. He waited until they . . . began to eat,"[41] and the plenitude of their meal intimates a newly attained shared duration. All of which seems substantiated when the baker "waited until they . . . began to eat," for this waiting now seems to be a time that is always already fulfilled, as if in a time, as Levinas puts it, that was "subordinated to eternity, to a present which neither passes nor can be gone beyond . . ." a "timeless ideality which exists unmoving above the immediate temporality of human patience, in the substitution of dialectical rigor for 'incompressible,' unavoidable, insurmountable *durée*."[42]

The baker waited, and yet the time of his waiting – and this is not a function of brevity, not a matter of time – does not have to be endured either in hours or minutes, or in the solitude of self. Ann's desperate projection of a time before its divisions into life and death, or mother and child, or self and other, has here, in Carver's tenderly implicit style, come true – if only for a time. If the sharing of a meal is the most ancient, intimate, and communal way of being in time, its ideality consists in its complete, communal, human embodiment that leaves no remainder lost or waiting.

# In Closing

For the last decade or so, I have volunteered on Bucknell's admissions day to give a talk to visiting students and their parents about Robert Frost's famous little poem "Stopping by Woods on a Snowy Evening." Lately, I have added Wordsworth's sonnet "Composed Upon Westminster Bridge" in which, as in Frost's poem, a traveler stops and sees, as if for the first time, a landscape wholly transformed. The condition for such seeing is in both poems what constitutes the poetic itself: an interruption of time, a stopping, a waiting, a lingering. In Frost's poem this stopping comes about with a sense of chaste illicitness as the traveler seems to look over his shoulder, hoping that the owner of the woods "will not see me stopping here / To watch his woods fill up with snow." Wordsworth announces in the second line of his poem that he "who could pass by / A sight so touching in its majesty" would be "dull . . . of soul." Not to pass by, to wait, to arrest the purposeful journey, is of course a Romantic trope whose cliché, take time to smell the roses, has been reiterated *ad nauseam*. Nevertheless, I usually end my talk by pointing out that our own allegorical journey through life attains value and perspective largely through the kind of stopping practiced in art or in a liberal arts education, and that one would hope not-passing-by would eventually become a habit of the soul. In our time of instant gratification, such habits are, of course, ever more illicit, our souls perhaps ever more dull.

Neither Frost nor Wordsworth claims instrumental purpose for the poetic. The poetic is not a function of some other purpose; the poetic does not serve to advance the traveler except in that Romantic idealistic way in that it may give the dull soul a moral inclination. The parents in my audience might, of course, want to be cautioned that Frost's traveler has veritably to yank himself out of his trance in the last three lines, which might not bode well for their offspring. A liberal education might likewise endanger the promising engineer or the dutiful economist. There is, as the dark night of the soul in Frost's poem intimates, something risky about waiting to watch the woods fill up with snow. One might never keep one's promises. One might become enamored – a possibility in Wordsworth's poem – with a utopian vision of life, "All bright and glittering in the smokeless air," that redeems it from its worldly grime. Even without its seductions, such waiting, such lingering, as in Frost or Wordsworth, remains at odds with a culture whose privileging of speed, industry, utility, and productivity imposes on life the infamous economic paradigm: time is money. This paradigm, I have suggested in this book, has led to a denigration of those experiences that require the kind of deliberate stopping – of economic time – that poems and works of art perform and require of us. It is only in such moments that we resist, or at least delay, what Jeanette Winterson has called "money culture."

In this book, I have argued that waiting can be a rewarding experience, eliciting reflection on time and human existence, and that waiting is an essential condition for aesthetic and ethical values. In waiting, we become – if often uncomfortably

– attuned to what Bergson calls the melody of duration that runs its course within us. This attunement, I hope to have shown, can be consciously practiced and valued. Waiting, as Simone Weil aptly puts this, is attention.

In the first two chapters, I tried to capture the elusive temporality of duration that, as soon as it is thought, becomes measurable, objectified clock time. But waiting is more than a certain *amount* of time, it is *experienced* time. We get up, we pace, we check our watches to escape this intimacy of time. A book on waiting must pay homage to Homer's Penelope, who waits no fewer than twenty years for her husband, and to Beckett's Vladimir and Estragon, who, for all we know, are still waiting. I have briefly discussed *Waiting for Godot* only to emphasize the subject of this book, which is waiting – not Godot. If Godot is the exemplary illusory object of waiting, Penelope is the exemplary waiter. In the last three years of her waiting, she develops a strategy to prolong her waiting by unraveling her weaving each night. Unlike the public account of her waiting that Penelope produces daily in her weaving, her nocturnal unweaving symbolizes the intimate, immeasurable aspects of waiting that are of primary concern in this book.



My claims that waiting is far from useless, that it is rather a fundamental constituent of our aesthetic and ethical abilities, are illustrated, and I hope substantiated, in Chapters five and six. Both of these chapters concerned themselves with artistic renderings of existential conditions – a poetic memory of life, a series of paintings about dying – each requiring of the reader or viewer a waiting that is wholly subservient to the temporality of the artistic presentation. In such waiting, we are removed not only from the time of clocks and the speed of modern life, but also from the ordinary expectations according to which waiting is supposed to be object-related and not in itself a valuable experience. But in reading a poem or in looking at a painting, I have argued, we find ourselves in the realm of duration, in the otherworldly temporality of the work of art – Frost's lovely, dark, and deep woods – that requires of us a waiting without object or end.

In the last chapter, I took up the distinction between time and duration that structured my philosophical argument in the first chapter and applied those two temporalities to an examination of waiting in a hospital setting. Here, the temporality of waiting expanded to include despair and hope. These, I hope to have shown, are the deepest experiences of duration; they cannot be reverted into the measurable dimensions of clock time.

The general argument of this book is that waiting is not a passage of time to be traversed but a condition of our being. In waiting, time enters our bodies; we are the time that passes. We wait even if we are not aware that we are waiting. The instrumental nature of ordinary waiting – where we usually wait for something that is supposed to be better than waiting – conceals this intimate, existential aspect of waiting. Waiting, in other words, is an opportunity to encounter those aspects of life deeply, perhaps neurotically, hidden in our busyness. If we claim our experience of waiting rather than being merely subjected to it, we resist the commercialization of time, we own our time, we make time matter – we matter. In waiting, in listening to the inward melody of duration, we become attuned to our being.

# Notes

## ONE NOBODY LIKES TO WAIT

1 St. Augustine, *Confessions*, trans. R.S. Pine-Coffin (Harmondsworth: Penguin, 1961), 264 (11.14).

2 In his *A Philosophy of Boredom* (London: Reaktion, 2005), Lars Svendsen claims similarly that his subject is equally indefinable.

3 Adam Phillips, *On Kissing, Tickling, and Being Bored: Psychoanalytic Essays on the Unexamined Life* (Cambridge, MA: Harvard University Press, 1993), 76.

4 Jean Giraudoux, *Électre* (Paris: Grasset, 1987), 92 (my translation).

5 Friedrich Nietzsche, *On the Genealogy of Morals and Ecce Homo*, trans. Walter Kaufman (New York: Vintage, 1989), 47.

6 Jeanette Winterson, *Art Objects: Essays on Ecstasy and Effrontery* (London: Vintage, 1996), 90, 190.

7 See Svendsen, *A Philosophy of Boredom*: "Boredom lacks the charm of melancholy . . . ." 19.

8 Simone Weil, *Waiting for God*, trans. Emma Craufurd (New York: Perennial Classics, 2001), 63.

9 Isaac Newton, *The Principia*, trans. Andrew Motte (New York: Promethius, 1995), 13.

10 D. Graham Burnett, "Mapping Time: Chronometry on Top of the World," *Daedalus* (Spring 2003): 14.

11 Sylviane Agacinski, *Time Passing: Modernity and Nostalgia*, trans. Jody Gladding (New York: Columbia University Press, 2003), 6.

12 Georg Simmel, *The Philosophy of Money*, trans. Tom Bottomore, David Frisby, and Kaethe Mengelberg (London: Routledge, 2004), 444–445.

13 Hence Beardsworth's observation that ". . . all experiences of time (including the 'a-temporal' temporalities of the unconscious) are to be

situated within processes of technicisation . . ." and ". . . the profit-related interest of capital is nothing but the reduction of the future to a minimal difference with the present . . . ." Richard Beardsworth, "Practices of Procrastination," *Parallax* 5, 1 (1999): 11, 12.

14 Richard C. Larson, "There's More to a Line Than Its Wait," *Technology Review* 91, 5 (July 1988): 60.

15 Winterson, *Art Objects*, 138, 139.

16 Martin Luther King, "Letter from Birmingham Jail," in *Why We Can't Wait* (New York: Harper & Row, 1964), 83.

17 Paul Virilio, *Negative Horizon: An Essay in Dromoscopy*, trans. Michael Degener (London: Continuum, 2005), 120, 122.

18 Robert J. Samuelson, "The Sad Fate of the Comma," *Newsweek* (July 23, 2007): 41.

19 *The Paul Virilio Reader*, ed. Steve Redhead (New York: Columbia University Press, 2004), 142.

20 Paul Virilio, *The Art of the Motor*, trans. Julie Rose (Minneapolis: University of Minnesota Press, 1995), 35.

21 Paul Virilio, *Negative Horizon*, 121.

22 Hartmut Rosa, "Social Acceleration: Ethical and Political Consequences of a Desynchronized High-Speed Society," *Constellations* 10, 1 (2003): 6–7, 9.

23 Ann Barr Snitow, "Mass Market Romance: Pornography for Women is Different," in *Feminist Literary Theory*, ed. Mary Eagleton (Oxford: Blackwell, 1997), 193.

24 Hugh Kenner, *Samuel Beckett: A Critical Study* (Berkeley: University of California Press, 1973), 14.

25 Samuel Beckett, *Waiting for Godot* (London: Faber and Faber, 2006), 27, 31.

26 Richard Gilman, "The Waiting Since," in *Samuel Beckett's Waiting for Godot*, ed. Harold Bloom (New York: Chelsea House Publishers, 1987), 68.

27 Marya Mannes, "Two Tramps," in *Casebook on Waiting for Godot*, ed. Ruby Cohn (New York: Grove Press, 1967), 30.

28 Norman Mailer, "A Public Notice on *Waiting for Godot*," in *Casebook*, ed. Cohn, 71.

29 Alain Robbe-Grillet, "Samuel Beckett or Presence on the Stage," in *Casebook*, ed. Cohn, 18.

30 Robert Champigny, "*Waiting for Godot*: Myth, Words, Wait," in *Casebook*, ed. Cohn, 143.
31 Theodor W. Adorno, "Trying to Understand *Endgame*," trans. Michael J. Jones, in *The Adorno Reader*, ed. Brian O'Connor (Oxford: Blackwell Publishers, 2000), 331.
32 Beckett, *Godot*, 29.
33 Hugh Kenner, in *Samuel Beckett's Waiting for Godot*, ed. Bloom, 61, 62.
34 Ibid., 60.
35 Beckett, *Godot*, 69.
36 Adorno, "Trying to Understand *Endgame*," 329.
37 Beckett, *Godot*, 16.
38 Ibid., 31.

## TWO A BRIEF THEORY OF WAITING

1 Henri Bergson, *Time and Free Will*, trans. F.L. Pogson (Mineola, NY: Dover Publications, 2001), 115.
2 Henri Bergson, *Duration and Simultaneity*, in *Henri Bergson: Key Writings*, ed. Keith Ansell Pearson and John Mullarkey (London: Continuum, 2002), 207.
3 Henri Bergson, *Creative Evolution* (New York: Cosimo, 2005), 12–13.
4 Henri Bergson, *Oeuvres* (Paris: Presses Universitaires de France, 1963), 502.
5 Bergson, *Duration and Simultaneity*, 216.
6 Bergson, *Oeuvres*, 502.
7 Henri Bergson, *The Creative Mind: An Introduction to Metaphysics*, trans. Mabelle L. Andison (Mineola, NY: Dover Publications, 2007), 113.
8 Ibid., 125.
9 Bergson, *Time and Free Will*, 100–1.
10 Bergson, *Duration and Simultaneity*, 205. Lyotard states similarly that "All genuine music . . . [a]spires to exemption from syntheses, forms, becomings, intentions and retentions . . . ." Jean-François Lyotard, *The Inhuman: Reflections on Time*, trans. Geoffrey Bennington and Rachel Bowlby (Stanford: Stanford University Press, 1991), 163.
11 Bergson, *The Creative Mind*, 123.
12 Walter Benjamin, "The Story Teller," in *Illuminations*, trans. Harry Zohn (New York: Schocken Books, 1968), 91.
13 Bergson, *The Creative Mind*, 123.

14 T.S. Eliot, *The Complete Poems and Plays* (London: Faber and Faber, 1969), 17.

15 Ibid., 173.

16 Ibid., 180.

17 Adorno, "Trying to Understand *Endgame*," 329.

18 Bergson, *Time and Free Will*, 129.

19 Wallace Stevens, *Collected Poems* (London: Faber and Faber, 2006), 288.

20 Bergson, *Creative Evolution*, 14

21 Bergson, *Time and Free Will*, 128.

22 We will encounter such a child in Chapter three.

23 Lars Svendsen writes similarly and with allusion to Bergson: "In boredom, time becomes 'refractory' because it will not pass like [*sic*] it usually does, and this is why the reality of time can be experienced" (128).

24 "If . . . this relation is so important to our well-being," as Leccardi notes, "how can one keep a social time that is increasingly rapid and fragmented together with the richness and the specific tempo of inner time?" Carmen Leccardi, "Resisting 'Acceleration Society,' " *Constellations* 10, 1 (2003): 39.

25 Beckett, *Godot*, 48.

26 Lawrence Harvey, "Art and the Existential in *Waiting for Godot*," in *Casebook*, ed. Cohn, 154.

27 Bergson, *The Creative Mind*, 102.

28 Ibid., 103.

29 As would Bergson's artist whose "senses or whose consciousness are less adherent to life" and who thus intuits a thing "for itself" (*The Creative Mind*, 162).

30 Rainer Maria Rilke, "The Ninth Elegy," in *The Selected Poetry of Rainer Maria Rilke*, trans. Stephen Mitchell (New York: Vintage, 1989), 199–201.

31 Bergson, *Creative Evolution*, 12.

32 Bergson, *The Creative Mind*, 75.

33 Eliot, *The Complete Poems*, 188.

34 Sylviane Agacinski, *Time Passing: Modernity and Nostalgia*, trans. Jody Gladding (New York: Columbia University Press, 2003), 60.

35 Simon Critchley, *Very Little . . . Almost Nothing* (London: Routledge, 2005), xxiv.

36 Quoted in ibid., 167.

37 Bergson, *Creative Evolution*, 18.

38 Bergson, *The Creative Mind*, 123.

39 Ibid., 125.

40 Henri Bergson, *Matter and Memory*, trans. Nancy Margaret Paul and W. Scott Palmer (Mineola, NY: Dover Publications, 2004), 27–28

41 Ibid., 59.

42 In their introduction to *Henri Bergson: Key Writings*, Pearson and Mullarkey point out that this claim is explicit in Bergson's later writings, whereas in *Time and Free Will* he had considered the question whether external things endure as indeterminate (10).

43 "Now, if living beings are, within the universe, just 'centres of indetermination,' and if the degree of this indetermination is measured by the number and rank of their functions, we can conceive that their mere presence is equivalent to the suppression of all those parts of objects in which their functions find no interest. They allow to pass through them, so to speak, those external influences which are indifferent to them; the others isolated, become 'perceptions' by their very isolation." Bergson, *Matter and Memory*, 28–29.

44 Ibid., 29.

45 Ibid., 30.

46 Bergson, *Creative Evolution*, 14.

47 Benjamin, "The Work of Art in the Age of Mechanical Reproduction," in *Illuminations*, 236, 237.

48 Bergson, *Creative Evolution*, 18.

49 Rilke, "The Eighth Elegy," in *The Selected Poetry*, 195, 197.

50 Rilke, *Die Gedichte* (Frankfurt: Insel Verlag, 1987), 869 (my translation).

51 E.M. Cioran, *A Short History of Decay*, trans. Richard Howard (New York: Arcade Publishing, 1998), 14.

52 Bergson, *The Creative Mind*, 124.

## THREE IN THE WAITING ROOM

1 Bergson, *The Creative Mind*, 139.

2 Elizabeth Bishop, *The Complete Poems* (New York: Farrar, Straus, and Giroux, 1983), 159–161.

3 Henry James, *The Wings of the Dove* (Harmondsworth: Penguin, 1978), 5. All further quotations, unless otherwise noted, are from this page.

4 Ibid., 8.

5 I am indebted to Pauline Fletcher for these words.

6 Eliot, *The Complete Poems*, 15.

7 Ibid., 23.

8 Ibid., 68.

9 In his book *Very Little . . . Almost Nothing*, Simon Critchley similarly notes that Beckett's materialism expresses itself in "forlorn particulars: refrigerators, bicycles, tape recorders, dustbins and pap" (xxiv).

10 Adorno, "Trying to Understand *Endgame*," 330.

11 Bergson, *Matter and Memory*, 44.

12 Laura Tanner, *Lost Bodies: Inhabiting the Borders of Life and Death* (Ithaca: Cornell University Press, 2006), 120, 121.

13 Bergson, *Time and Free Will*, 132.

14 Ibid., 133.

15 Ibid., 134.

16 M.A.R. Habib, *The Early T.S. Eliot and Western Philosophy* (Cambridge: Cambridge University Press, 1999), 86.

17 Bergson, *Time and Free Will*, 134.

18 Winterson, *Art Objects*, 90.

19 Agacinski, *Time Passing*, 55.

20 Eliot, *The Collected Poems*, 17, 173.

21 Maurice Blanchot, *Faux Pas*, trans. Charlotte Mandell (Stanford: Stanford University Press, 2001), 113.

22 Ibid., 112.

## FOUR PENELOPE'S INSOMNIA

1 All book and line references in the text are from Homer, *The Odyssey*, trans. Robert Fitzgerald (New York: Vintage, 1990).

2 Maurice Blanchot, "Waiting," in *The Blanchot Reader*, ed. Michael Holland (Oxford: Blackwell, 1995), 273.

3 See Thomas L. Dumm, "Resignation," *Critical Inquiry* 25 (Autumn 1998), particularly the section "Waiting (The Exile of Words)": 75–76.

4 Roland Barthes, *A Lover's Discourse*, trans. Richard Howard (New York: Hill and Wang, 1994), 38.

5 Louise Glück, *Meadowlands* (Hopewell: Ecco Press, 1996), 15.

6 Louise Glück, *The Seven Ages* (New York: HarperCollins, 2002), 27.

7 Jean Pierre Vernant, "Odysseus in Person," *Representations* 67 (Summer 1999): 185.

8 Glück, *Meadowlands*, 42.

9 Hans-Jost Frey, *Interruptions*, trans. Georgia Albert (Albany: SUNY Press, 1996), 57.

10 Ibid., 57.

11 Maurice Blanchot, *The Gaze of Orpheus and Other Literary Essays*, trans. Lydia Davis (Barrytown, NY: Station Hill, 1981), 104.

12 Vernant, "Odysseus in Person," 26.

13 Michael N. Nagler, "Dread Goddess Revisited," in *Reading the Odyssey: Selected Interpretive Essays*, ed. Seth L. Schein (Princeton: Princeton University Press, 1996), 152.

14 I.D. Jenkins, "The Ambiguity of Greek Textiles," *Arethusa* 18, 2 (1985): 114.

15 Nancy Felson-Rubin, *Regarding Penelope: From Characters to Poetics* (Princeton: Princeton University Press, 1994), 37.

16 Margaret Visser, *The Geometry of Love* (New York: North Point, 2000), 31.

17 Jenkins, "Ambiguity of Greek Textiles," 113.

18 See John Donne, "A Valediction: Forbidding Mourning," in *Selected Poems*, ed. James Reeves (London: Heinemann, 1974). In this poem, the woman is famously the fixed foot of a compass. "Yet when the other far doth rome, / It leanes, and hearkens after it . . . ."

19 Stevens, "The World as Meditation," in *Collected Poems*, 455.

20 Rosanna Warren, "Odyssey," *American Poetry Review* 35, 6 (Nov.–Dec. 2006): 48.

21 Leccardi, "Resisting 'Acceleration Society,' " 38.

22 Blanchot, *The Gaze of Orpheus*, 95.

23 Bergson, *Time and Free Will*, 129.

24 Frank Kermode, *The Sense of an Ending: Studies in the Theory of Fiction* (London: Oxford University Press, 1966), 47.

25 Maurice Blanchot, *The Infinite Conversation*, trans. Susan Hanson (Minneapolis: University of Minnesota Press, 1993), 121 (*La conversation infinie*, 176).

26 Benjamin, "The Image of Proust," in *Illuminations*, 202.

27 Gérard Genette, "Order in Narrative," in *Literature in the Modern World*, ed. Dennis Walder (Oxford: Oxford University Press, 1990), 151. This seems to me a different kind of autonomy than that mentioned by Hans-Georg Gadamer in *The Relevance of the Beautiful* (Cambridge: Cambridge University Press, 1986), where Gadamer speaks of "fulfilled

or autonomous time" which is a characteristic of the festival and the work of art (42).

28 Benjamin, "The Image of Proust," 203.

29 See Andrew Gibson, *Towards a Postmodern Theory of Narrative* (Edinburgh: Edinburgh University Press, 1996), where Gibson exemplifies postmodern narrative *parcours* with *The Odyssey* (17, see also 204).

30 Blanchot, *Faux Pas*, 250.

31 Virginia Woolf, *The Waves* (New York: Harcourt Brace, 1978), 21–22.

32 Felson-Rubin, *Regarding Penelope*, 37.

33 Ann Smock, "Conversation," in *Maurice Blanchot: The Demand of Writing*, ed. Carolyn Bailey Gill (London: Routledge, 1996), 128.

34 Georg Lukács, *Die Theorie des Romans* (München: dtv, 1994), 108. Within its formalized "eternity," Lukács argues, "time stands still" and the protagonist moves and acts in "several dimensions and no particular direction" always assured of his or her place in a diviner spectacle. Thus in *The Odyssey*, according to Lukács and quite contrary to this argument, "time and duration have no reality" (my translation).

35 Italo Calvino, "The Odysseys within *The Odyssey*," in *The Uses of Literature*, trans. Patrick Creagh (New York: Harcourt Brace, 1986), 142. Calvino points out other mutualities between Odysseus and Penelope, such as their similiar use of "trickery" and "counterfeiting."

36 Ibid., 137.

37 Paul Ricoeur, *Memory, History, Forgetting*, trans. Kathleen Blamey and David Pellauer (Chicago: University of Chicago Press, 2004), 151.

38 Frederick Ahl and Hanna M. Roisman, *The Odyssey Reformed* (Ithaca: Cornell University Press, 1996), 31.

39 Benjamin, "The Storyteller," in *Illuminations*, 101.

40 Jean-Paul Sartre, *"What is Literature?" and Other Essays* (Cambridge, MA: Harvard University Press, 1988), 50.

41 Kermode, *The Sense of an Ending*, 8.

42 Although the futility of Penelope's weaving is proverbial – Socrates likens her "labouring in vain" (*Phaedo* 84a) to the soul's imprisonment in emotions – I argue here quite to the contrary that only the ending of her weaving would condemn her work to futility.

43 Peter Brooks, *Reading for the Plot: Design and Intention in Narrative* (Cambridge, MA: Harvard University Press, 1992), 111. "[F]ulfillment must be

delayed so that we can understand it in relation to origin and to desire . . . ."

44 Theodor Adorno, *Aesthetic Theory*, trans. C. Lenhardt (London: Routledge, 1984), 21.

45 Brooks, *Reading for the Plot*, 109–110.

46 Uvo Hölscher, "Penelope and the Suitors," in *Reading the Odyssey*, ed. Schein, 135. Hölscher comments: "This scene has alienated interpreters since antiquity. It seemed unworthy of the majestic, 'circumspect' Penelope: *Regina prope ad meretricias artes descendit* [the queeen descends nearly to the arts of a courtesan] was the often-cited judgment of scholarship."

47 Sartre, *What is Literature?* 49.

48 Ibid., 52.

49 Hans-Georg Gadamer, *The Relevance of the Beautiful and Other Essays*, trans. Nicholas Walker (Cambridge: Cambridge University Press, 1986), 45.

## FIVE LINGERING, TARRYING, DWELLING UPON

1 Gadamer, *The Relevance of the Beautiful and other Essays*, 45. The German text reads: "*Es geht in der Erfahrung der Kunst darum, dass wir am Kunstwerk eine spezifische Art des Verweilens lernen. Es ist ein Verweilen, das sich offenbar dadurch auszeichnet, dass es nicht langweilig wird. Je mehr wir verweilend uns darauf einlassen, desto sprechender, desto vielfältiger, desto reicher erscheint es. Das Wesen der Zeiterfahrung der Kunst ist, dass wir zu weilen lernen. Das ist vielleicht die uns zugemessene endliche Entsprechung zu dem, was man Ewigkeit nennt.*" Hans-Georg Gadamer, *Die Aktualität des Schönen* (Stuttgart: Reclam, 1977), 60.

2 *Gadamer in Conversation*, ed. and trans. Richard E. Palmer (New Haven: Yale University Press, 2001), 77.

3 Hans-Georg Gadamer, *Wahrheit und Methode (Truth and Method): Grundzüge einer philosophischen Hermeneutik* (Tübingen: J.C.B. Mohr, 1986), 75. Gadamer writes similarly that "Every experience is 'a moment of the infinite life.' " Or: "Just as experience is part of the totality of life, so also is that totality present in the individual experience." Thus the temporality of the work of art and that of the experience (*Erlebnis*) are structurally similar. While our tarrying in the work of art is indeterminate, objectless, purposeless thus intuiting eternity, our sense of time in an ordinary experience seems more directional and purposeful thus intuitive of Bergsonian duration: "*Die durch seinen intentionalen Gehalt bestimmte Einheit des*

*Erlebnisses steht . . . in einer unmittelbaren Beziehung zum Ganzen, zur Totalität des Lebens. Bergson spricht von representation des Ganzen . . .*" (75). But the metaphysical – rather than existential – dimensions of duration are also claimed by Bergson who assigns our intuition of duration two destinies: "downward or upward," material or metaphysical. Upward ". . . would be," Bergson writes, "a living and consequently still moving eternity where our own duration would find itself like the vibrations of light . . ." (*The Creative Mind*, 158).

4 Weil, *Waiting for God*, 63.

5 Lloyd Schwartz and Sybil P. Estess, eds. *Elizabeth Bishop and Her Art* (Ann Arbor: University of Michigan Press, 1983), 295.

6 Ibid., 289.

7 Bishop, *Complete Poems*, 176.

8 Ibid., 11. The little painting in "Poem" appears thus as a corrective of a painting in an earlier poem which bears the telling title, "Large Bad Picture" (see also Schwartz and Estess, *Elizabeth Bishop*, 314).

9 Bishop, "The Monument," 23.

10 Bishop, "Sandpiper," 131.

11 Schwartz and Estess, *Elizabeth Bishop*, 41.

12 Bishop, "The Fish," 42.

13 Gadamer, *Wahrheit und Methode*, 76.

14 Bergson, *The Creative Mind*, 158.

15 Ibid., 135.

16 Schwartz and Estess, *Elizabeth Bishop*, 288.

17 Bergson, *Duration and Simultaneity*, in *Key Writings*, 216.

18 Theodor W. Adorno, *Minima Moralia: Reflections from Damaged Life*, trans. E.F.N. Jephcott (London: New Left Books, 1974), 76.

19 Ibid., 76.

20 Agacinski, *Time Passing*, 55.

21 Elaine Scarry, *On Beauty and Being Just* (Princeton: Princeton University Press, 1999), 18.

22 Ibid., 58.

23 Bergson, *Duration and Simultaneity*, in *Key Writings*, 216.

24 Bergson, *Creative Evolution*, 98.

25 Adorno, *Minima Moralia*, 76.

26 Ibid., 77.

27 Scarry, *On Beauty and Being Just*, 18.

28 Adorno, *Aesthetic Theory*, 122–123.

29 Walter Benjamin, *The Arcades Project*, trans. Howard Eiland and Kevin McLaughlin (Cambridge, MA: Belknap Press, 1999), 427.

30 Adorno, *Aesthetic Theory*, 323.

31 Mikel Dufrenne, *The Phenomenology of Aesthetic Experience*, trans. Edward S. Casey *et al.* (Evanston: Northwestern University Press, 1973), 25.

32 Weil, *Waiting for God*, 63.

33 Adorno, *Minima Moralia*, 77.

34 Bishop, "The Moose," 172.

35 Adorno, *Minima Moralia*, 228.

36 Ibid., 228.

37 Dufrenne, *Phenomenology of Aesthetic Experience*, liv.

## SIX WAITING FOR DEATH

1 Weil, *Waiting for God*, 64.

2 Emmanuel Levinas, *Entre Nous: Thinking-of-the-Other*, trans. Michael B. Smith and Barbara Harshav (New York: Columbia University Press, 1998), 224.

3 Weil, *Waiting for God*, 64.

4 Blanchot, *The Infinite Conversation*, 121 (*La conversation infinie*, 176).

5 Ibid., 121.

6 Weil, *Waiting for God*, 64–65.

7 Sharon L. Hirsh, *Ferdinand Hodler* (New York: George Braziller, 1982), 122.

8 Blanchot, *The Infinite Conversation*, 121.

9 Hirsh, *Ferdinand Hodler*, 126.

10 *Ferdinand Hodler, 1853–1918*, ed. Jura Brüschweiler and Guido Magnaguagno (Zürich: Kunsthaus Zürich, 1983), 319.

11 Levinas, *Entre Nous*, 217.

12 Ibid., 94.

13 Ibid., 167.

14 Elisabeth Bronfen, *Over Her Dead Body: Death, Femininity and the Aesthetic* (New York: Routledge, 1992). In her discussion of this sequence of paintings, Bronfen argues that the "withdrawal [of these images] from any semantically fixed encoding, such as the labelling 'beautiful' or 'horrible' would imply, entails not only their fascination. It is precisely this 'instability' which also allows for a conceptual entrance into the

interstice of violence and the production of images" (45). Her subsequent claims, however, do not sustain this instability and seem unequivocal in their insistence on the images' aesthetic erasure of "the real" and of "the feminine body": "The 'closure' that occurs at the end of the image sequence can be read as a triumph, a resurrection of the dead woman by the mourning painter" (46) – whose paintings in subsequent pages are "to fulfil his mourning through painting this body, [which] looks like an expropriation of the feminine body, a reduction of this body to an object externally coded; an act, furthermore, marking the site of his prowess, his imagination, his creativity" (50).

15 *Ferdinand Hodler*, ed. Brüschweiler and Magnaguagno, 370.

16 Blanchot, *The Infinite Conversation*, 121.

17 Levinas, *Entre Nous*, 167.

18 Ibid., 168.

19 Blanchot, *The Infinite Conversation*, 121.

20 Alain P. Toumayan, *Encountering the Other: The Artwork and the Problem of Difference in Blanchot and Levinas* (Pittsburgh: Duquesne University Press, 2004), 122.

21 Levinas, *Entre Nous*, 169.

22 Hirsh, *Ferdinand Hodler*, 124.

23 *Ferdinand Hodler*, ed. Brüschweiler and Magnaguagno, 319.

24 Levinas, *Entre Nous*, 169.

25 Ibid., 93.

26 Ibid., 170.

27 Ibid., 170.

28 Ibid., 227.

29 Ibid., 231.

30 Emmanuel Levinas, "Reality and Its Shadow," in *The Continental Aesthetics Reader*, ed. Clive Cazeaux (New York: Routledge, 2000), 117–18.

31 Ibid., 119.

32 Ibid., 126.

33 Levinas, *Entre Nous*, 11.

34 Ibid., 170.

35 The term "violence," denoting as it does real events suffered by real people, might be as liable to erase their suffering as might the "rhetorical violence" that Bronfen attributes to Hodler's images. This seems

most explicitly the case when Bronfen equates the violence of death with the violence of rhetoric: ". . . we are dealing either with a violent decomposition of a female body through cancer or with a violent rhetoric which effaces the real pain through an allegorising gaze." Bronfen, *Over Her Dead Body*, 51.

36 Levinas, *Entre Nous*, 167.

37 Ibid., 170.

38 Ibid., 10.

39 Bronfen, *Over Her Dead Body*, 51.

40 Levinas, *Entre Nous*, 224.

41 Ibid., 217.

## SEVEN WAITING AND HOPING

1 Raymond Carver, "Poseidon and Company," in *Call If You Need Me: The Uncollected Fiction and Other Prose* (New York: Vintage, 2001), 156.

2 Ibid., 157.

3 Raymond Carver, *Where I'm Calling from: New and Selected Stories* (New York: Atlantic Monthly Press, 1988), 282.

4 Ibid., 282–283.

5 Ibid., 287.

6 Blanchot, *The Infinite Conversation*, 121.

7 Tanner, *Lost Bodies*, 65.

8 Carver, *Where I'm Calling from*, 283.

9 Bergson, *Time and Free Will*, 129.

10 Carver, *Where I'm Calling from*, 285.

11 Ibid., 285–289.

12 Ibid., 286.

13 Ibid., 284.

14 Ibid., 285.

15 Carver, Ibid., 285.

16 Blanchot, *The Infinite Conversation*, 44 (*La conversation infinie*, 63).

17 Ibid., 44.

18 Carver, Ibid., 285.

19 Ibid., 289.

20 Ibid., 289.

21 Levinas, *God, Death, and Time*, trans. Bettina Bergo (Stanford: Stanford University Press, 2000), 55.

22 Blanchot, The Infinite Conversation, 44.
23 Levinas, *God, Death, and Time*, 67.
24 Blanchot, The Infinite Conversation, 121.
25 Ibid., 121.
26 Carver, *Where* I'm Calling from, 289.
27 Ibid., 288.
28 Frey, Interruptions, 57.
29 Carver, *Where* I'm Calling from, 288.
30 Ibid., 288.
31 Ibid., 288.
32 Ibid., 288.
33 Ibid., 280.
34 Ibid., 301.
35 Ibid., 301.
36 Weil, *Waiting* for God, 63.
37 Carver, *Where* I'm Calling from, 291.
38 Ibid., 301.
39 Ibid., 288.
40 Ibid., 288.
41 Ibid., 301.
42 Levinas, Entre Nous, 137–8.

# Works Cited

Adorno, Theodor W. *Minima Moralia: Reflections from Damaged Life*. Translated by E.F.N. Jephcott. London: New Left Books, 1974.

—— *Aesthetic Theory*. Translated by C. Lenhardt. London: Routledge & Kegan Paul, 1984.

—— "Trying to Understand *Endgame*." Translated by Michael J. Jones. In *The Adorno Reader*. Edited by Brian O'Connor. Oxford: Blackwell Publishers, 2000.

Agacinski, Sylviane. *Time Passing: Modernity and Nostalgia*. Translated by Jody Gladding. New York: Columbia University Press, 2003.

Ahl, Frederick, and Hanna M. Roisman. *The Odyssey Reformed*. Ithaca: Cornell University Press, 1996.

Augustine. *Confessions*. Translated by R.S. Pine-Coffin. Harmondsworth: Penguin, 1961.

Barthes, Roland. *A Lover's Discourse*. Translated by Richard Howard. New York: Hill and Wang, 1994.

Beardsworth, Richard. "Practices of Procrastination." *Parallax* 5, 1 (1999): 10–12.

Beckett, Samuel. *Waiting for Godot*. London: Faber and Faber, 2006.

Benjamin, Walter. *Illuminations: Essays and Reflections*. Translated by Harry Zohn. New York: Schocken, 1968.

—— *The Arcades Project*. Translated by Howard Eiland and Kevin McLaughlin. Cambridge, MA: Belknap Press, 1999.

Bergson Henri. *Oeuvres*. Paris: Presses Universitaires de France, 1963.

—— *Time and Free Will*. Translated by F.L. Pogson. Mineola, NY: Dover Publications, 2001.

—— *Duration and Simultaneity*. In *Henri Bergson: Key Writings*. Edited by Keith Ansell Pearson and John Mullarkey. London: Continuum, 2002.

—— *Key Writings*. Edited by Keith Ansell-Pearson and John Mullarkey. London: Continuum, 2002.
—— *Matter and Memory*. Translated by Nancy Margaret Paul and W. Scott Palmer. Mineola, NY: Dover Publications, 2004.
—— *Creative Evolution*. New York: Cosimo, 2005.
—— *The Creative Mind: An Introduction to Metaphysics*. Translated by Mabelle L. Andison. Mineola, NY: Dover Publications, 2007.
Bishop, Elizabeth. *The Complete Poems*. New York: Farrar, Straus and Giroux, 1983.
Blanchot, Maurice. *L'Attente l'oubli*. Paris: Gallimard, 1962.
—— *The Gaze of Orpheus and Other Literary Essays*. Translated by Lydia Davis. Barrytown, NY: Station Hill, 1981.
—— *The Infinite Conversation*. Translated by Susan Hanson. Minneapolis: University of Minnesota Press, 1993.
—— "Waiting." In *The Blanchot Reader*. Edited by Michael Holland. Oxford: Blackwell, 1995.
—— *Faux Pas*. Translated by Charlotte Mandell. Stanford: Stanford University Press, 2001.
Bloom, Harold, ed. *Samuel Beckett's Waiting for Godot*. New York: Chelsea House, 1987.
Bronfen, Elisabeth. *Over Her Dead Body: Death, Femininity and the Aesthetic*. New York: Routledge, 1992.
Brooks, Peter. *Reading for the Plot: Design and Intention in Narrative*. Cambridge, MA: Harvard University Press, 1992.
Brüschweiler, Jura, and Guido Magnaguagno, eds. *Ferdinand Hodler, 1853–1918*. Zürich: Kunsthaus Zürich, 1983.
Burnett, D. Graham. "Mapping Time: Chronometry on Top of the World." *Daedalus* (Spring 2003): 5–19.
Calvino, Italo. "The Odysseys within *The Odyssey*." In *The Uses of Literature*. Translated by Patrick Creagh. New York: Harcourt Brace, 1986.
Carver, Raymond. *Where I'm Calling from: New and Selected Stories*. New York: Atlantic Monthly Press, 1988.
—— *Call If You Need Me: The Uncollected Fiction and Other Prose*. New York: Vintage, 2001.
Champigny, Robert. "*Waiting for Godot*: Myth, Words, Wait." In *Casebook on Waiting for Godot*. Edited by Ruby Cohn. New York: Grove Press, 1967.

Cioran, E.M. *A Short History of Decay*. Translated by Richard Howard. New York: Arcade Publishing, 1998.

Cohn, Ruby, ed. *Casebook on Waiting for Godot*. New York: Grove Press, 1967.

Critchley, Simon. *Very Little . . . Almost Nothing: Death, Philosophy, Literature*. London: Routledge, 2004.

Dante, Alighieri. *The Inferno*. Translated by Allen Mandelbaum. Toronto: Bantam Books, 1980.

Donne, John. "A Valediction: Forbidding Mourning." In *Selected Poems*. Edited by James Reeves. London: Heinemann, 1974.

Dufrenne, Mikel. *The Phenomenology of Aesthetic Experience*. Translated by Edward S. Casey *et al*. Evanston: Northwestern University Press, 1973.

Dumm, Thomas L. "Resignation." *Critical Inquiry* 25 (Autumn 1998): 56–76.

Eliot, T.S. *The Complete Poems and Plays*. London: Faber and Faber, 1969.

Felson-Rubin, Nancy. *Regarding Penelope: From Characters to Poetics*. Princeton: Princeton University Press, 1994.

Frey, Hans-Jost. *Interruptions*. Translated by Georgia Albert. Albany: SUNY Press, 1996.

Gadamer, Hans-Georg. *Die Aktualität des Schönen*. Stuttgart: Reclam, 1977.

—— *The Relevance of the Beautiful and Other Essays*. Translated by Nicholas Walker. Cambridge: Cambridge University Press, 1986.

—— *Wahrheit und Methode: Grundzüge einer philosophischen Hermeneutik*. Tübingen: J.C.B. Mohr, 1986.

*Gadamer in Conversation: Reflections and Commentary*. Edited and translated by Richard E. Palmer. New Haven: Yale University Press, 2001.

Genette, Gérard. "Order in Narrative." In *Literature in the Modern World*. Edited by Dennis Walder. Oxford: Oxford University Press, 1990.

Gibson, Andrew. *Towards a Postmodern Theory of Narrative*. Edinburgh: Edinburgh University Press, 1996.

Gilman, Richard. "The Waiting Since." In *Samuel Beckett's Waiting for Godot*. Edited by Harold Bloom. New York: Chelsea, 1987.

Giroudoux, Jean. *Électre*. Paris: Grasset, 1987.

Glück, Louise. *Meadowlands*. New York: Ecco, 1996.

—— *The Seven Ages*. New York: Ecco, 2002.

Habib, M.A.R. *The Early T.S. Eliot and Western Philosophy*. Cambridge: Cambridge University Press, 2006.

Harvey, Lawrence. "Art and the Existential in Waiting for Godot." In *Casebook on Waiting for Godot*. Edited by Ruby Cohn. New York: Grove Press, 1967.

Hirsh, Sharon L. *Ferdinand Hodler*. New York: George Braziller, 1982.

Hodler, Ferdinand. *Ferdinand Hodler, 1853–1918*. Ed. Jura Brüschweiler and Guido Magnaguagno. Zürich: Kunsthaus Zürich, 1983.

Hölscher, Uvo. "Penelope and the Suitors." In *Reading the Odyssey: Selected Interpretive Essays*. Edited by Seth L. Schein. Princeton: Princeton University Press, 1996.

Homer. *The Odyssey*. Translated by Robert Fitzgerald. New York: Vintage, 1990.

James, Henry. *The Wings of the Dove*. Harmondsworth: Penguin, 1978.

Jenkins, I.D. "The Ambiguity of Greek Textiles." *Arethusa* 18, 2 (1985): 109–132.

Kenner, Hugh. *Samuel Beckett: A Critical Study*. Berkeley: University of California Press, 1973.

—— "Waiting for Godot." In *Samuel Beckett's Waiting for Godot*. Edited by Harold Bloom. New York: Chelsea, 1987.

Kermode, Frank. *The Sense of an Ending: Studies in the Theory of Fiction*. London: Oxford University Press, 1966.

King, Martin Luther, Jr. "Letter from Birmingham Jail." In *Why We Can't Wait*. New York: Harper & Row, 1964.

Larson, Richard C. "There's More to a Line Than Its Wait." *Technology Review* 91, 5 (1988): 60–67.

Leccardi, Carmen. "Resisting 'Accelaration Society.' " *Constellations* 10, 1 (2003): 34–41.

Levinas, Emmanuel. *Entre Nous: Thinking-of-the-Other*. Translated by Michael B. Smith and Barbara Harshav. New York: Columbia University Press, 1998.

—— *God, Death, and Time*. Translated by Bettina Bergo. Stanford: Stanford University Press, 2000.

—— "Reality and Its Shadow." In *The Continental Aesthetics Reader*. Edited by Clive Cazeaux. New York: Routledge, 2000.

Lukács, Georg. *Die Theorie des Romans*. München: dtv, 1994.

Lyotard, Jean-François. *The Inhuman: Reflections on Time*. Translated by Geoffrey Bennington and Rachel Bowlby. Stanford: Stanford University Press, 1991.

Mailer, Norman. "A Public Notice on *Waiting for Godot*." In *Casebook on Waiting for Godot*. Edited by Ruby Cohn. New York: Grove Press, 1967.

Mannes, Marya. "Two Tramps." In *Casebook on Waiting for Godot*. Edited by Ruby Cohn. New York: Grove Press, 1967.

Merwin, W.S. *The Vixen*. New York: Knopf, 1998.
Nagler, Michael N. "Dread Goddess Revisited." In *Reading the Odyssey: Selected Interpretive Essays*. Edited by Seth L. Schein. Princeton: Princeton University Press, 1996.
Newton, Isaac. *The Principia*. Edited by Andrew Motte. New York: Prometheus, 1995.
Nietzsche, Friedrich. *On the Genealogy of Morals and Ecce Homo*. Translated by Walter Kaufman. New York: Vintage, 1989.
Phillips, Adam. *On Kissing, Tickling, and Being Bored: Psychoanalytic Essays on the Unexamined Life*. Cambridge, MA: Harvard University Press, 1993.
Redhead, Steve, ed. *The Paul Virilio Reader*. New York: Columbia University Press, 2004.
Ricoeur, Paul. *Time and Narrative*. Vol. 1. Translated by Kathleen McLaughlin and David Pellauer. Chicago: University of Chicago Press, 1984.
—— *Memory, History, Forgetting*. Translated by Kathleen Blamey and David Pellauer. Chicago: University of Chicago Press, 2004.
Rilke, Rainer Maria. *Die Gedichte*. Frankfurt: Insel Verlag, 1987.
—— *The Selected Poetry of Rainer Maria Rilke*. Translated by Stephen Mitchell. New York: Vintage, 1989.
Robbe-Grillet, Alain. "Samuel Beckett or Presence on the Stage." In *Casebook on Waiting for Godot*. Edited by Ruby Cohn. New York: Grove Press, 1967.
Rosa, Hartmut. "Social Acceleration: Ethical and Political Consequences of a Desynchronized High-Speed Society." *Constellations* 10, 1 (2003): 3–33.
Samuelson, Robert J. "The Sad Fate of the Comma." *Newsweek*. July 23, 2007.
Sartre, Jean-Paul. *"What is Literature?" and Other Essays*. Cambridge, MA: Harvard University Press, 1988.
Scarry, Elaine. *On Beauty and Being Just*. Princeton: Princeton University Press, 1999.
Schwartz, Lloyd and Sybil P. Estess, eds. *Elizabeth Bishop and Her Art*. Ann Arbor: University of Michigan Press, 1983.
Simmel, Georg. *The Philosophy of Money*. Translated by Tom Bottomore, David Frisby, and Kaethe Mengelberg. London: Routledge, 2004.
Smock, Ann. "Conversation." In *Maurice Blanchot: The Demand of Writing*. Edited by Carolyn Bailey Gill. London: Routledge, 1996.
Snitow, Ann Barr. "Mass Market Romance: Pornography for Women is Different." In *Feminist Literary Theory*. Edited by Mary Eagleton. Oxford: Blackwell, 1997.

Stevens, Wallace. *Collected Poems*. London: Faber and Faber, 2006.

Svendson, Lars. *A Philosophy of Boredom*. Translated by John Irons. London: Reaktion, 2005.

Tanner, Laura. *Lost Bodies: Inhabiting the Borders of Life and Death*. Ithaca: Cornell University Press, 2006.

Toumayan, Alain P. *Encountering the Other: The Artwork and the Problem of Difference in Blanchot and Levinas*. Pittsburgh: Duquesne University Press, 2004.

Vernant, Jean Pierre. "Odysseus in Person." *Representations* 67 (Summer 1999): 1–33.

Virilio, Paul. *The Art of the Motor*. Translated by Julie Rose. Minneapolis: University of Minnesota Press, 2004.

—— *Negative Horizon: An Essay in Dromoscopy*. Translated by Michael Degener. London: Continuum, 2005.

Visser, Margaret. *The Geometry of Love*. New York: North Point, 2000.

Warren, Rosanna. "Odyssey." *American Poetry Review* 35, 6 (Nov.–Dec. 2006).

Webster, Augusta. *Portraits and Other Poems*. Edited by Christine Sutphin. Peterborough, Canada: Broadview, 2000.

Weil, Simone. *Waiting for God*. Translated by Emma Craufurd. New York: Perennial Classics, 2001.

Winterson, Jeanette. *Art Objects: Essays on Ecstasy and Effrontery*. London: Vintage, 1996.

Woolf, Virginia. *The Waves*. New York: Harcourt Brace, 1978.

# Index

# Related titles from Routledge

## On Film

### Second Edition

Stephen Mulhall

Reviews of the first edition:

'Mulhall's philosophical discussion of each film is highly stimulating. A provocative and engaging book which makes for stimulating reading for anyone interested in both film and philosophy.' – *Matthew Kieran, Philosophical Books*

'the themes he identifies as central-most crucially, a concern with human embodiment and thus, with both human generativity and mortality-are explored convincingly, even brilliantly at times...Despite the amount of closely argued material which is packed into a relatively short book, the clarity and precision of the writing make it something of a page-turner.' – *Deborah Thomas, European Journal of Communication*

In this significantly expanded new edition of his acclaimed exploration of the relation between philosophy and film, Stephen Mulhall broadens the focus of his work from science fiction to the espionage thriller and beyond.

The first part of the book discusses the four *Alien* movies. Mulhall argues that the sexual significance of the aliens themselves, and of Ripley's resistance to them, takes us deep into the question of what it is to be human. These four chapters develop a highly original and controversial argument that films themselves can philosophize – a claim Mulhall expands upon and defends in part two of this book, before applying his interpretative model to another sequence of contemporary Hollywood movies: the *Mission: Impossible* series.

A new chapter is devoted to each of the three films in that series, discussing them in the context of other films by the relevant directors. In this discussion, the nature of television becomes as central a concern as the nature of cinema, and this shift in genre also makes room for a detailed reading of Spielberg's *Minority Report*.

*On Film*, Second Edition is essential reading for anyone interested in philosophy, film theory and cultural studies, and in the way philosophy can enrich our understanding of cinema.

**Stephen Mulhall** is Fellow and Tutor in Philosophy at New College, Oxford, and author of *Heidegger and* Being and Time (Routledge) and *The Conversation of Humanity*.

ISBN13: 978–0–415–44153–7 (pbk)
ISBN13: 978–0–203–92852–3 (ebk)

# Related titles from Routledge

## On Architecture

Fred Rush

Architecture is a philosophical puzzle. Although we spend most of our time in buildings, we rarely reflect on what they mean or how we experience them. With some notable exceptions, they have generally struggled to be taken seriously as works of art compared to painting or music and have been rather overlooked by philosophers.

In *On Architecture*, Fred Rush argues this is a consequence of neglecting the role of the body in architecture. Our encounter with a building is first and foremost a bodily one; buildings are lived-in, communal spaces and their construction reveals a lot about our relation to the environment as a whole.

Drawing on examples from architects classic and contemporary such as Le Corbusier and Frank Lloyd Wright, and exploring the significance of buildings in relation to film and music and philosophers such as Heidegger and Merleau-Ponty, Fred Rush argues that philosophical reflection on building can tell us something important about the human condition.

**Fred Rush** is Associate Professor of Philosophy at the University of Notre Dame, Indiana, USA. He is the editor of *The Cambridge Companion to Critical Theory*.

ISBN13: 978–0–415–39618–9 (hbk)
ISBN13: 978–0–415–39619–6 (pbk)